TREASURES OF WISDOM

Michael Routt

TREASURES OF WISDOM
Studies in Colossians & Philemon

HOMER A. KENT, JR.

BAKER BOOK HOUSE
Grand Rapids, Michigan

To
BECKY and GARY
whose home is founded on the ideals
of Colossians 3

Contents

Illustrations

Picture Credits

Levant Photo and Design Service, P. O. Box 1284, Santa Cruz, California 95060.
The Metropolitan Museum of Art, Fifth Avenue at 82nd Street, New York, New York 10028.

Abbreviations

Arndt	*A Greek-English Lexicon of the New Testament,* by William F. Arndt and F. Wilbur Gingrich
ASV	American Standard Version, 1901
EGT	*The Expositor's Greek Testament*
KJV	King James Version, 1611
LXX	Septuagint (Greek translation of the Old Testament)
NASB	New American Standard Bible, 1971
Nestle	Novum Testamentum Graece
NIV	New International Version, 1973
NT	New Testament
OT	Old Testament
TDNT	*Theological Dictionary of the New Testament*

Preface

The epistles of Paul to the Colossians and to Philemon have a relevance to current thought that makes them as fresh as the day they were written. Not too many years ago a treatise involving angels and the spirit world seemed far removed from modern life. One read with amusement and perhaps with an air of condescension of medieval monks arguing about how many angels could assemble on the point of a pin. Until recently, social issues were also far less explosive, and their relevance to Christian faith was not clearly seen.

Yet today concern about these issues has reached a fever pitch. Interest in the occult has greatly increased, and religious cults have mushroomed to exploit this interest. Human rights and social discrimination are topics that clamor for attention, occupying prominent places in government legislation and the news media, and affecting the conduct of daily life. A book on angels written by an evangelical from a biblical perspective was on the bestseller lists for months.

Every Christian can profit from a careful study of Colossians and Philemon, two epistles that speak to these very issues. It is my desire that readers will find in these letters of the apostle Paul the "treasures of wisdom" that are provided in Jesus Christ. Here can be found the safeguards against non-Christian currents that swirl about men today, both from the spirit world which is hostile to Christ, and from the less-than-Christian attitudes which too often mar our relations with our fellows.

I would like to express appreciation to two colleagues in the New Testament Department at Grace Theological Seminary, Dr. James L. Boyer and Professor John A. Sproule, who read the manuscript and gave valuable counsel regarding content and style. A special word of thanks is due also to Professor Robert D. Ibach, Jr., Librarian, for preparing the map.

Homer A. Kent, Jr.
Winona Lake, Indiana

The Epistle
to the Colossians

1

Introduction to Colossians

Tychicus was ready to leave Rome. His journey would take him eastward to his home in the Roman province of Asia (Acts 20:4) in what is today the land of Turkey. Years before, he had joined the missionary team of the apostle Paul, and would continue that close association throughout Paul's career (Titus 3:12, II Tim. 4:12). In recent days he had been with Paul in Rome, where the apostle was imprisoned awaiting the outcome of his appeal to Caesar. That imprisonment had already lasted for many months, and would ultimately extend to two full years (Acts 28:30). Now, however, it was time for Tychicus to depart for his field of responsibility. The task of the church must move forward; even the imprisonment of an apostle must not hinder its progress.

Communication by letter over long distances was not an easy matter in the first century. No postal system was available to ordinary citizens. It was necessary to find someone who was traveling to the desired destination, and then prevail upon him to deliver one's letter. Paul, therefore, seized the opportunity afforded by the trip of Tychicus to send three letters to churches in Asia—epistles to the Colossians, to Philemon, and to the Ephesians. Two of these—Colossians and Philemon—were sent to the same city. Although written nineteen centuries ago, the issues to which they spoke still confront mankind in various ways. Paul's answers are the Word of God to His church.

Authorship

Of the ancient records still available to us, Irenaeus (A.D. 140-203) is the earliest to quote the Epistle to the Colossians by name as the work of Paul. Irenaeus cited Colossians 4:14 in his statement: "Paul in the Epistle to the Colossians says, Luke the beloved physician greets. . . ."[1] Many other early writers also showed acquaintance with this epistle.[2]

From the epistle itself there are numerous indications that Paul was indeed the author. Some scholars have disputed the genuineness of the epistle, but they are clearly in the minority.[3] The evidence from the letter itself, as well as the strong early testimony from history, demonstrates beyond any reasonable doubt that the apostle Paul wrote this letter to the church at Colosse.

First, the writer calls himself Paul three times in the epistle (1:1, 23; 4:18). There is nothing suspicious about these references, and the burden of proof is on the critic to show why these statements should not be believed.

Furthermore, the language, style, and subject matter of Colossians is consistent with the other writings of Paul. The piling up of clauses to form extremely long sentences was characteristic of the apostle (see 1:3-8, 9-20). The number of new words (34), that is, words not found elsewhere in Paul's epistles, is not exceptional, and is largely accounted for by the peculiar heresy at Colosse that Paul was addressing. The statements about the person of Christ are consistent with what Paul taught in his other letters. Christ is shown to be the head of the body which is the church (1:18, cf. Eph. 1:22-23) and sovereign over all created things (1:15-17; cf. I Cor. 8:6; 15:24-28; Rom. 11:36).

The angelology in Colossians is in harmony with Pauline in-

---

1. Irenaeus, *Against Heresies*, 3.14.1, in *Ante-Nicene Fathers*, ed. Alexander Roberts and James Donaldson (Grand Rapids, reprinted 1950), I, 438.

2. Among them are Ignatius, Epistle of Barnabas, Justin Martyr, Theophilus of Antioch, Clement of Alexandria, Tertullian, Origen, and Marcion.

3. A concise resumé of this negative opinion is given by Donald Guthrie, *New Testament Introduction, The Pauline Epistles* (Chicago, 1961), pp. 167-71; and F. O. Francis, "Colossians," *The Interpreter's Dictionary of the Bible, Supplementary Volume*, ed. Keith Krim (Nashville, 1976), pp. 169-70.

struction in other passages.[4] References to angels may be found in Paul's letters to the Romans (8:38), Corinthians (I Cor. 6:3; 11:10; 15:24, 40), Galatians (1:8; 3:19), and Ephesians (1:21). The prominence of references to angels in Colossians can be accounted for by the false teaching at Colosse which Paul was refuting (Col. 2:18). It is not necessary to postulate a full-blown Gnosticism of the second century to account for the heretical opposition which the author confronted. It should not be forgotten that Jewish writings of this period also contained much angelology.

Finally, the Epistle to the Colossians is closely connected with the one to Philemon, which most scholars agree is a genuine epistle of Paul. Five of the persons named in Colossians 4:10-14 appear also in Philemon 23-24.[5] In both letters, Timothy was Paul's companion, Archippus was given a message, and Onesimus was mentioned as coming to Colosse. Hence there is no serious reason to reject the church's historical position that the Epistle to the Colossians has come down to us from the apostle Paul.

The Church at Colosse

The city of Colosse had been an important one as early as the fifth century B.C. The Greek historian Herodotus described it as "a great city in Phrygia" in 481 B.C.[6] Xenophon wrote of "Colossae, an inhabited city, prosperous and large."[7] It was located in the Lycus Valley, about one hundred miles east of Ephesus on the main east-west trade route from Ephesus. This route passed through Colosse and then branched at Apamea, one road leading to Syria and the other to the Euphrates.[8] In its more prosperous days Colosse had been an important center for

---

4. See A. S. Peake, "The Epistle to the Colossians," *The Expositor's Greek Testament*, ed. W. Robertson Nicoll (Grand Rapids, reprint), III, 478-84.

5. Aristarchus, Marcus, Epaphras, Lucas, Demas.

6. *Herodotus*, VII, 30, trans. A. D. Godley, in the Loeb Classical Library (New York, 1922), III, 345.

7. Xenophon *Anabasis*, I.ii.6, trans. Carleton L. Brownson, in the Loeb Classical Library (New York, 1920), p. 253.

8. *The Wycliffe Historical Geography of Bible Lands*, ed. Charles F. Pfeiffer and Howard F. Vos (Chicago, 1967), pp. 316-17.

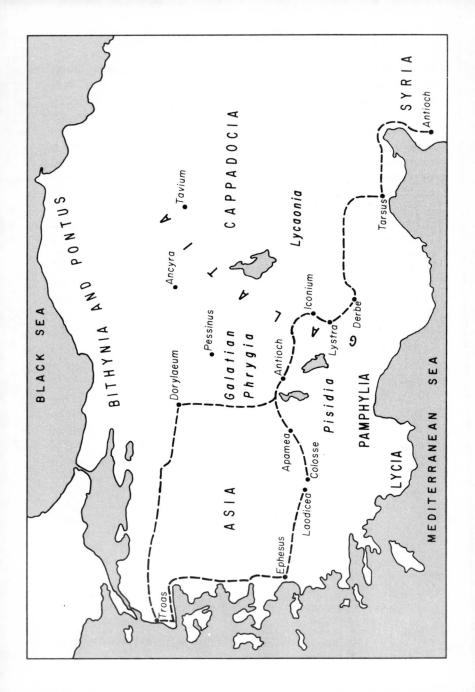

the production of woolen goods. By New Testament times, however, Colosse had dwindled, being outstripped by the neighboring cities Hierapolis and Laodicea. The three settlements were close enough geographically to have much contact, and all are mentioned in the epistle (2:1; 4:13, 16).

Colosse is not mentioned in the Book of Acts as one of the cities Paul visited. That fact, coupled with certain statements in the epistle, has raised a question about Paul's relation to this congregation. Had he ever visited Colosse? Was he the founder of the church there?

Favoring the conclusion that Paul had been in Colosse is the fact that he did make two visits to Phrygia (a part of the province of Asia) on his second and third missionary journeys (Acts 16:6; 18:23), and it would have been natural for him to take the road which passed through Colosse. Furthermore, the apostle had friends at Colosse. He revealed his acquaintance with Philemon, Apphia, Archippus, Onesimus, and Epaphras, and showed that he had a rather intimate knowledge of their situation (4:7-18). Some of the friends named above may have been recent ones, but Philemon, who resided at Colosse, appears to have been a convert of Paul from an earlier time (4:9; cf. Philem. 19).

Even if Paul did pass through the city, however, it still is not certain that he founded the church, and certain factors seem to indicate that he did not. There were other routes which Paul could have taken, and Acts 16:6 specifically states that he was forbidden by the Holy Spirit to preach in Asia on the second journey. In the Acts account of the third journey, Paul is described as making his way to Ephesus by way of the "upper coasts" (Acts 19:1), which may refer to the higher-lying route rather than the lower level valley road through Colosse.[9]

Certain statements in Colossians also indicate that Paul had not personally founded the church there. In 2:1, Paul groups his

9. William M. Ramsay, *St. Paul the Traveller and the Roman Citizen* (Grand Rapids, reprinted 1949), pp. 265.

Fig. 1. Asia Minor, showing Roman provinces, cities, and major highways.

readers with the Laodiceans and others who had "not seen my face in the flesh." Furthermore, the apostle's comment in 1:4 that he had "heard" of their faith and love,[10] coupled with his remark in 1:8 that Epaphras had conveyed such information to him, suggests that Paul had not been personally present. In addition, Epaphras is clearly stated to have been the one from whom the Colossians had learned the gospel (1:5-7).

It could be, however, that the church was actually organized as a result of Paul's long teaching ministry in Ephesus (Acts 19:10), and was later led by Epaphras who had been trained by Paul. This would explain why the apostle felt responsible in some degree for the oversight of the Colossians and wrote them this letter. The conversion of Philemon and his family could have come about through a visit of Philemon to Paul at Ephesus, or perhaps if Paul passed through Colosse before the church was organized, or even through the testimony of Paul's protégé, Epaphras. In any of these circumstances, Paul could accurately have said to Philemon, "Thou owest unto me even thine own self besides" (Philem. 19).

All things considered, it is best to regard Colossians as a letter written to a church that Paul did not personally establish. He regarded it as looking to him for guidance because it had been established by Epaphras, who was perhaps a student Paul had trained at Ephesus. In any event, no barrier of strangeness separated the author from his readers. He felt deep concern over their problems, and sought to win their full allegiance to the truth of God as fully as he did in the churches where he had personally labored.

The Occasion and Date

Two circumstances caused Paul to write the companion letters to the Colossians and Philemon. One was the visit and report of Epaphras, who brought news of the Colossians and informed Paul about certain problems confronting the church (1:7-8). That report had been generally favorable, but the doctrinal danger

---

10. This statement cannot be pressed apart from the context, however, for Paul wrote similarly regarding the Ephesians whom he had obviously known personally (Eph. 1:15).

was sufficiently disturbing that Paul wished to grapple with it at once before it made inroads among the Colossian believers. Some erroneous teachings are best dealt with by ignoring them (I Tim. 4:7), for their own weakness will cause them to fail. Others are more serious and should be respected for the danger they pose. Paul regarded the "Colossian heresy" as potentially disastrous, for its various features were sufficiently attractive to offer some appeal to almost everyone. To those who were impressed by ritual, it offered the rites and ceremonies of Moses. To the mystically inclined it advocated angel worship. And to the philosophically minded, there was the religious appeal of asceticism, which suggests spirituality to many. Hence Paul used the occasion to protect the Colossians against this religious falsehood which could threaten their "order and the stedfastness of your faith in Christ" (2:5).

The second circumstance which prompted Paul to write was the situation with Onesimus (4:9). This runaway slave had been converted to Christ, and was now willing to return to Colosse and to his defrauded master Philemon. If he returned in the company of Tychicus, he would be safe from the slave catchers who were always on the lookout for such persons. However, his Christian master would need a reliable explanation of the circumstances in order to respond in a truly Christian manner. Paul took advantage of the trip Tychicus was about to make, and wrote with both these circumstances in mind (4:7-9).

The traditional view that Paul wrote both letters during his first Roman imprisonment continues to fit the circumstances better than any other explanation. Paul was imprisoned in Rome for two years (A.D. 59-61); Rome would have provided concealment for a runaway slave. Paul had more freedom to preach at Rome than during his other imprisonments, a circumstance which fits Colossians 1:28-29 and 4:2-4 (cf. Acts 28:30-31; *contra* 24:23). A date around A.D. 60 or 61 is therefore suggested.

Special Features

The Epistle to the Colossians has certain distinctive features which the Bible student should recognize.

1. Colossians is one of the four Prison Epistles of Paul.

Whenever Paul's writings are classified, the four that were written during his first imprisonment in Rome are grouped under this heading. Each letter states that the writer was in prison at the time. The four are Ephesians (3:1; 4:1; 6:20), Philippians (1:7, 13, 14, 16-17), Colossians (4:3, 18), and Philemon (1, 9, 10).

2. Colossians was one of three epistles delivered on the same trip by Tychicus. Colossians, Philemon, and Ephesians were all sent from Rome to churches in Asia Minor, and were carried by Paul's associate who himself came from Asia (Acts 20:4). It is certain that Tychicus, the bearer of Colossians (4:7), also delivered the letter to Philemon on the same trip since the return of Onesimus (Philem. 10-12) is mentioned in Colossians (4:7-9). Tychicus is also indicated as the bearer of Ephesians (6:21), and the similarity of the epistles makes it likely that all were written at the same time and delivered together.

3. Colossians is a companion epistle to Philemon. The church at Colosse apparently met in the house of Philemon, the owner of Onesimus (Philem. 2). Both letters were thus sent to Colosse, and both mentioned Onesimus and Archippus (Col. 4:9, 17; Philem. 2, 10).

4. The Colossian church had apparently been founded and pastored by Epaphras (Col. 1:7; 4:12; Philem. 23). This man had come to' Rome with news for Paul, but was not at that time returning to Colosse.

5. Colossians also bears a close relationship to the Epistle to the Ephesians. Many passages in the two epistles are parallel. Following is a list of some examples where the wording as well as the thought is similar:

Colossians	Ephesians
1:3-4	1:15-17
1:14	1:7
1:18	1:22
1:20	1:10
1:21	2:1, 12
1:25	3:2
1:27	1:18
2:13	2:5
2:19	4:15-16
3:8-9	4:22
3:10	4:24

Colossians	Ephesians
3:16	5:19
3:18—4:2	5:22—6:9
4:2	6:18
4:7-8	6:21-22

These similarities, however, are not the kind of wooden repetitions which would suggest that one letter was a copy of the other. They are rather the similarity of phrasing which a writer could easily employ when he wrote two letters dealing with several common subjects, and wrote them at about the same time.

6. The Colossian heresy was different from other false teaching reflected in the New Testament. (Paul's epistles often indicate the doctrinal errors which confronted his converts.) Galatians contains Paul's refutation of the Judaizing efforts being put forth to force Gentile Christians under the jurisdiction of the Mosaic law. In the Thessalonian epistles Paul endeavored to clarify his readers' understanding of the second coming of Christ, and the status of Christians who have died. In the Corinthian epistles, a tendency to sensuality was denounced by the apostle.

In Colosse, however, a religious philosophy appeared on the scene which contained elements not specifically mentioned in Pauline discussions elsewhere. To be sure, the philosophy contained Jewish elements (2:16) as did the false teaching in Galatia, but it also had an aspect of angel worship (2:18) and a strong ascetic emphasis (2:20-23). Angel worship and asceticism were never part of normative Judaism, although contemporary Jewish literature did contain an elaborate angelology, and some extreme Jewish groups did adopt an ascetic way of life. These elements did not seem to be significant in the earlier troubles in Galatia, but were an integral part of the heretical teaching which Paul refuted in his Epistle to the Colossians.

7. The identity of the "letter to the Laodiceans," mentioned in Colossians 4:16, remains uncertain. It appears to be a letter which Paul wrote to the church in that neighboring city.[11] The

---

11. The interpretation that "the epistle from Laodicea" refers to a letter from the Laodiceans to Paul, rather than from Paul to the Laodiceans, causes contextual difficulties. If the former were correct, the letter would be in Paul's possession and he could send it to the Colossians himself.

apostle apparently desired that the two churches should share their respective letters with each other.

Various attempts have been made to identify this epistle. An apocryphal work appeared in the early church called the Epistle to the Laodiceans, consisting of a collection of Pauline phrases strung together. However, it is absent from all early Greek manuscripts of the New Testament, and its appearance in Latin versions has not been found earlier than the sixth century. This document was certainly not the object of Paul's reference.

Others have identified it as the letter which we designate as the epistle to the Ephesians. It is true that three ancient manuscripts omit the words "in Ephesus" (Eph. 1:1), and the possibility remains that our canonical Ephesians could have been intended for a wider readership. However, there is no conclusive proof for this identification. No manuscripts have ever been found with the name "Laodicea" instead of "Ephesus" in Ephesians 1:1.

The best answer at present is that this "letter to the Laodiceans" has been lost. Perhaps the contents were not of permanent significance, and therefore the church recognized that this particular letter was not "God-breathed" (II Tim. 3:16). We know of at least one other letter Paul wrote which was lost (I Cor. 5:9). The biblical doctrine of the inspiration of Scripture does not require us to believe that everything which an apostle wrote was holy Scripture. The "lost letter" to the Corinthians is one example (I Cor. 5:9); the "letter to the Laodiceans" is apparently another.

The Outline of Colossians

Greeting (1:1-8)
 A. The Writer (1:1)
 B. The Addressees (1:2)
 C. The Thanksgiving (1:3-8)
I. Explanation of the Person and Work of Christ (1:9-29)
 A. The Prayer Based on Christ (1:9-14)
  1. The Occasion (1:9a)
  2. The Petitions (1:9b-12)
  3. The Basis (1:13-14)

Questions for Discussion

1. Who founded the church at Colosse?

2. What previous contacts did Paul have with the church at Colosse and its individual members?
3. What circumstances prompted Paul to write Colossians and Philemon?
4. What are some distinguishing features of the Epistle to the Colossians?
5. Why do Colossians and Ephesians have sections which are so similar?

2

A Greeting to the Believers

COLOSSIANS 1:1-8

Those familiar with Paul's epistles take special notice of the introductory greetings he uses in addressing his readers. They are typical of letters written in that day, containing the author's name, the destination, and a word of salutation. But Paul's letters do not use time-worn clichés. Each greeting is suited to the particular audience in view, and is thus distinct from others. Comparison of Paul's various introductions makes this clear; each letter was a fresh statement from the author's heart. No wooden repetition of pious phrases mars the impression one receives that this letter to the Colossians (and all his other letters) sprang from the total concentration of the author upon a particular group of people and the needs of a specific congregation.

GREETING (1:1-8)

A. The Writer (1:1)

VERSE 1. Paul identified himself by referring to his *position* as "apostle of Christ Jesus." To this congregation which he had not personally founded (see Introduction), it was appropriate that the writer use this full title to state his authority. An "apostle" was a duly commissioned delegate or messenger with authorization to represent someone else. In Paul's case, he was an "apostle of Christ Jesus."[1] What Paul had to say to the Colossians was actually a message from his Lord. This title "apostle of Christ Jesus" is clearly not shared with Timothy; it must refer to something Paul possessed but which Timothy did not. Although the designation "apostle" is sometimes used more widely in the New Testament,[2] the formal title "apostle of Christ Jesus" seems to be reserved for the Twelve plus Paul. It was in this restricted sense that Paul wrote to the Colossians, most of whom had never seen him, to give an authoritative explanation of the person and work of Christ, and to point out the errors which were being propagated in their midst.

Paul's *appointment* to his apostleship had come about by God's intention. It was not the result of personal ambition, a fine education, parental guidance, or encouragement from friends. Rather, it occurred by the will of God who had planned it from beginning to end (Gal. 1:1, 15). God had directly intervened in Paul's life, had turned him around from the course in which he was heading, and had granted him a revelation of the glorified Jesus with a commission to proclaim the gospel (Acts 9:6, 15-16). Paul's absolute certainty that his appointment was the will of God enabled him to remain unswayed by even the most discouraging circumstances. He had come to know the will of God for his life, and that relegated every other circumstance to a secondary position.

The author's *associate* is introduced as "Timothy the brother." Timothy's name is joined with Paul's in the introductory greetings of II Corinthians, Philippians, I and II Thessalonians, and Philemon, as well as Colossians. Two of Paul's epistles are addressed to Timothy, and he is also mentioned in Romans, I Corinthians, and Hebrews. This prominent associate of the apostle was with Paul at the time of writing, and may have

1. The United Bible Societies Greek text (UBS), regarded as the best by many scholars, employs this word order of the names rather than "Jesus Christ" as given in the KJV.

2. For example, Barnabas is included in the category as a member of Paul's apostolic missionary party (Acts 14:4, 14). Epaphroditus is called the Philippians' apostle (Phil. 2:25). James the Lord's brother is mentioned in close association with the apostle Peter in terms that could imply that he also was an apostle in the wider sense (Gal. 1:18-19). See my discussion in *The Freedom of God's Sons* (Grand Rapids, 1976), p. 47.

known some of the Colossian Christians, just as Paul did. However, Timothy did not qualify for the title of apostle in the same sense as Paul did. Therefore, the author designated him as "the brother," an honorable title which acknowledged Timothy as a true Christian brother, a sharer along with Paul of new life from their heavenly Father. Paul used this same terminology "the brother" to describe Quartus (Rom. 16:23), Sosthenes (I Cor. 1:1), Apollos (I Cor. 16:12), and an unnamed person (II Cor. 8:18; 12:18).

It must not be supposed, however, that Timothy was a co-writer of the letter. The plural "we" is dropped after 1:9, and Paul is clearly indicated as the sole writer of the letter in such passages as 1:23-25, 29; 4:18, and many others.

B. The Addressees (1:2)

VERSE 2. The addressees are first described in terms of their spiritual *position*. They are "the saints and faithful brothers in Christ." Several grammatical features need to be recognized in this expression. First, the employment of only one article "the" means that "saints" and "faithful brothers" are not two separate groups but are simply two designations of the same persons.

Second, the word translated as the noun "saints" (*hagiois*) can also be treated as the adjective "holy." Thus the translation "holy and faithful brothers" is possible. Two factors, however, argue against that usage here. Paul uses the same word in his introductions in II Corinthians, Ephesians, and Philippians, where it must have the sense of the noun "saints." Furthermore, in the very next sentence Paul uses the word again where it clearly means "saints" (Col. 1:4). Hence it is best to understand that Paul is describing his readers' spiritual position as being "set apart" (the basic meaning of the word) by God to Himself, a position that is enjoyed by every Christian, not just a few "super holy" persons. They are also addressed as "faithful brothers," a reference that indicated their personal character demonstrated steadfastness of faith in their new lives as part of the Christian brotherhood.

The readers are next described in terms of their *geographical*

Fig. 2. The mound of Colosse, view east. *Levant*

location. They lived "in Colosse," a city of Phrygia which was incorporated into the Roman administrative unit known as the province of Asia. Its nearest neighbors were the cities of Laodicea (eleven miles west) and Hierapolis (thirteen miles northwest), which are also mentioned in the letter (2:1; 4:13, 15, 16). The three cities were located in the valley of the Lycus River, which flowed through Colosse.

The fact that Colosse, Laodicea, and Hierapolis are not mentioned in the Book of Acts is a reminder that Acts does not describe the full scope of growth of the Christian movement. There were undoubtedly many other churches existing during that time which are not described in Acts. The author of Acts had to be selective as he depicted the march of the gospel from Jerusalem to Rome. He focused on certain key centers where Paul labored in his career, but there must have been many smaller places like Colosse where the gospel made its impact, lives were changed, and churches were established.

The *blessing* bestowed upon the Colossians by Paul consisted of the twin benefits of grace and peace. Paul has adapted a familiar Greek greeting[3] and coupled it with the regular Hebrew

3. Letters in Greek commonly began with *chairein* ("greetings," Acts 15:23; James 1:1), which Paul regularly transforms to *charis* ("grace").

salutation, "peace" (*šalom*). As a Christian expression Paul used the terms to denote the Father's[4] gracious favor bestowed upon men without regard to merit, and to indicate the inner assurance, the sense of spiritual health, which enables the believer to be content even in the midst of turmoil.

C. The Thanksgiving (1:3-8)

1. The Nature of the Thanksgiving (1:3)

VERSE 3. The gratitude Paul felt for the Colossians was expressed in prayer to God. The apostle knew full well that the transformation in their lives had occurred because God had worked among them. Paul never let the visible successes of his ministry or those of others obscure his perspective. Paul knew that God is the One who is ultimately responsible, and to Him belongs our unending gratitude. Consequently, most of Paul's epistles begin with a thanksgiving to God for what has been accomplished.[5]

As the apostle states his thanks, he identifies God as "Father of our Lord Jesus Christ." There can be no better Christian identification of God than this. In Old Testament times a frequent designation was "the God of Abraham, of Isaac, and of Jacob" (Exod. 3:6, 16), for this related God to the Jewish patriarchs to whom God had revealed Himself in a direct way. In the Christian era, however, God has revealed Himself in His unique Son, so that Christ could say, "He that hath seen me hath seen the Father" (John 14:9).

In this verse, the word "always" should be connected with the phrase "we give thanks" rather than with the word "praying." The author does not mean that he and Timothy were always praying for the Colossians (surely there were times when other tasks occupied them), but rather that they always gave thanks whenever they *did* pray for the Colossians. The meaning is: "We always give thanks when engaged in praying for you." Something of Paul's greatness of heart is reflected here. He al-

---

4. Many ancient manuscripts omit the additional words "and the Lord Jesus Christ" which are in the Textus Receptus and are found in the KJV. Most modern versions regard the additional words as a scribal alteration to make this passage conform to similar statements in Eph. 1:2, Phil. 1:2, etc.

5. The only exceptions are II Corinthians, Galatians, I Timothy, and Titus.

ways found matters for which to thank God whenever the church at Colosse came to his mind. He did not let their problems, their weaknesses, and their failures dim his view of the entire picture. He never forgot what God had accomplished in their midst and would continue to perform in days to come.

2. *The Occasion of the Thanksgiving* (1:4)

VERSE 4. What prompted Paul's outpouring of gratitude to God was the report which he and Timothy had received about the spiritual progress of the Colossians. "Having heard of your faith" would be a literal rendering of Paul's phrase, and it doubtless refers to the information brought by Epaphras (1:8).

Two matters were prominent in this report from Colosse. One was the Colossians' "faith in Christ Jesus." Paul made it clear that biblical faith involves not just intellectual assent to a creed but trust and commitment as well. Hence Paul had been assured that the Colossians had truly put their trust for eternal life in the saving work of Christ.

Special notice should be taken of the phrase "in Christ Jesus" (*en Christōi Iēsou*). The preposition "in" (*en*) is not the usual one employed in the Greek New Testament for placing one's faith initially in Christ for salvation.[6] It is a word which more commonly depicts the sphere in which something exists or operates. Hence Paul is speaking here of the Colossians' continued demonstration of faith as they lived in the sphere of a vital spiritual union with Christ. Their original belief in Christ had produced lives which continued to trust Him for all of their needs and for the fulfillment of every promise.

The second matter of interest in the report from Colosse was the "love" which the Christians were displaying toward "all the saints." The faith which had brought each one into a life-sharing union with Christ also created a spiritual brotherhood among all the believers. This love (*agapēn*) was no mere emotional attraction, but an attitude which the Spirit of God produced in believers (Gal. 5:22). It caused them to desire what was best for others, and made them willing to sacrifice their own interests in favor of what would benefit their fellows (John 15:13; I Cor. 13).

---

6. The usual prepositions after *pistis* ("faith") and *pisteuō* ("believe") are *eis* or *epi*.

The greatest example was given by Jesus Himself, who challenged His followers to emulate Him (John 13:34-35; 15:12). In Colossians, this love is particularly focused upon the mutual relations of Christians. Paul does not infer that believers should be unconcerned about the non-Christians around them, but that as members of a spiritual brotherhood they have a special responsibility to their "family"; for this he commends them.

3. The Explanation of Their Condition (1:5-8)

VERSE 5. Paul's thanksgiving to God was based upon an accurate assessment of the Colossians' spiritual condition. He not only knew what progress they had made in their Christian lives, but he also understood why and how it had been accomplished. He said, first of all, it was due to the *hope* laid away for them in heaven (1:5a). It was this which had prompted their love and their continuing faith.[7] As they increasingly realized what God had already done and what promises were yet in store, their trust had deepened and their love for their brothers and sisters in Christ who were fellow-participants in these blessings had grown. This passage reveals that the Christian virtues of faith, hope, and love are intertwined. Each affects the other, and the growth of one causes an increase in the exercise of the others.

The word "hope" has both a subjective and an objective sense. It can describe an attitude of expectancy, and also can denote the object "hoped for." In the present instance the objective sense is the more applicable, for this hope is said to be laid away or reserved in heaven. Nevertheless the certainty of that future good (it is certain because God has promised it) creates a response of hopefulness, and this is what prompts an energetic display of Christian conduct on the part of alert and knowledgeable believers. These prospects of blessing reserved in heaven include our coming resurrection and glorification, release from sin and suffering, eternal bliss in heaven, and com-

---

7. Some relate the phrase "on account of the hope" (*dia tēn elpida*) back to "we give thanks" in verse 3, thus making the passage read, "We give thanks . . . for the hope which is laid up for you in heaven." But this seems awkward and unlikely, since Paul does not use the expression "we give thanks on account of" (*eucharistoumen dia*). Therefore, it is simpler and more logical to link the phrase with the words immediately preceding, making "the hope laid up for you in heaven" the explanation of the Colossians' faith and love.

pletion of everything that salvation has secured. It is all vested in Jesus Christ, who has already entered heaven as our forerunner (Heb. 6:19-20), and who is the very personification of our "blessed hope" (Titus 2:13).

Paul next explained that this Christian hope had become the Colossians' possession because of the gospel which they had heard (1:5b-6). This gospel was the message of good news which they "heard before." Before what? Not merely before the moment of writing (an obvious fact not needing any mention in the letter), but before the strange new teachings of Jewish ritual, angel worship, and asceticism had invaded the church at Colosse. This explanation fits the emphasis in the rest of the sentence where Paul stressed that the original message was contained "in the word of the truth of the gospel." The gospel, beginning with the life and work of Jesus Christ in the land of Israel, was now going forth into the rest of the world. It had reached Colosse, and had brought salvation to many of its people.

Verse 6. The apostle reminded his readers that they were part of a grand movement of God that was taking place throughout the world wherever the gospel had gone. There may be a subtle counterattack in this verse against the false teaching at Colosse. It is often the case that perverters of Christian truth convey the notion that they have an exclusive claim on some segment of God's truth, and that only they can impart the secret. Paul countered by saying that true believers are part of a spiritual brotherhood growing throughout the world, not just in one little portion of Asia Minor. "In all the world" is a legitimate hyperbole, not uncharacteristic of Paul (for other instances, see Rom. 1:8; 10:18; I Thess. 1:8). Surely the meaning is that the gospel was at that time going out into all the world without restriction. The task was yet incomplete (Paul did not say it was finished), but the point was that God had not limited the gospel to a certain few.

The older Greek manuscripts include the words "and increasing"[8] after "bearing fruit," and each of these expressions denotes a distinct idea. The idea that the gospel bears fruit

---

8. *kai auxanomenon*

describes its inherent power to create new life.[9] The metaphor seems to be drawn from our Lord's parables of the sower (Matt. 13:1-9) and of the seed growing by itself (Mark 4:26-29). Wherever the gospel went it proved itself to be "the power of God unto salvation" (Rom. 1:16) as it did its work in individual lives. "Increasing," on the other hand, describes the outward growth of the gospel. It not only produces its fruit in individuals, but continues to spread beyond its present limits. Evangelism is in view in this passage.

The experience occurring throughout the world wherever the gospel went was the very same phenomenon that the Colossians had witnessed in their midst. Nor was it a new experience for the Colossians, for it had begun when they first heard the gospel. They needed to break away from their more recent fascination with the new religious philosophy being promoted in their midst. They had to back off and recall what it really was that had transformed their lives. They needed to remember that they had been saved by hearing and receiving the gospel which was the announcement of "the grace of God in truth." This was far different from the human traditions (2:8) and decrees and legalistic practices (2:20) which some dangerous teachers were advocating. The gospel which had brought them hope was the good news that God had provided in His Son Jesus Christ everything they needed to receive righteousness and eternal life.

VERSE 7. The apostle concluded this thanksgiving by explaining that the hope which had been imparted through the gospel had occurred by the *ministry of Epaphras* (1:7-8). His relationship to the Colossians is first sketched. It was Epaphras who had caused them to learn the gospel, the true message of God's grace. The verb for "learn" is the root of the Greek noun "disciple." Epaphras had enlisted these people as learners, or disciples, and had become their teacher. This man is mentioned three times in the New Testament, and all of these references connect him with Colosse (Col. 1:7; 4:12; Philem. 23).[10]

---

9. The Greek middle here *karpophoroumenon* is commonly explained as connoting inherent energy, "bearing fruit of or for itself." Contrast the active form in 1:10.

10. There is no good reason to identify Epaphras with Epaphroditus except that the names are similar. Epaphroditus is always mentioned in connection with Philippi (Phil. 2:25; 4:18), and Epaphras with Colosse.

Epaphras had come to Rome with news for Paul, but was not returning to Colosse at this time (Col. 4:12). It is possible that he had become imprisoned himself, or more likely that he was so constant in his assistance to Paul that he merited the description "fellow prisoner" (Philem. 23).

Epaphras is next described in his relationship to Paul and Timothy as "our beloved fellow-servant." This description "fellow servant" is used of Tychicus in its only other New Testament occurrence (4:7). The word (*sundoulou*) marks Epaphras' position as the property of Christ, and as one who shared this relationship with Paul and Timothy (and Tychicus). They were bondslaves of Christ, not merely in the general sense that all Christians have been bought by Him (I Cor. 6:19-20), but in the more restricted sense of preachers and teachers of the gospel who have been commissioned for direct or special service. Inasmuch as Epaphras, Paul, and Timothy were fellow servants, any rejection of Epaphras by the Colossians in favor of the the heretical teachers would be a disowning of Paul and Timothy as well.

Paul then spoke of Epaphras in his relation to Christ. He was a "faithful minister of Christ." The word "minister" (*diakonos*) differs from the word "servant" (*doulos*) used above in that it connotes voluntary service. Both aspects of service characterize the effective servant of God. He willingly devotes himself to a ministry of helping others because he recognizes this to be the desire of his Master who has every right to direct him.

This faithful ministry of Epaphras had been performed "on our behalf" (NASB). Paul had been unable to go to Colosse with Timothy to fulfill his ministry as the apostle to the Gentiles. Consequently, Epaphras went as a substitute. A variation occurs among the ancient manuscripts at this point, and is reflected in the KJV translation "for you" instead of "on behalf of us." The reading adopted above has the support of the best Greek evidence, and is utilized in such newer versions as the NIV and NASB.[11]

---

11. It is surprising that the third edition of the United Bible Societies Greek New Testament adopts *humōn* ("you") rather than *hēmōn* ("us"), although admitting the superior Greek evidence for the latter. The editors were swayed by the evidence from the versions and patristic use (Bruce M. Metzger, *A Textual Commentary on the Greek New Testament* [London, 1971], pp. 619-20).

VERSE 8. When Epaphras made his report to Paul about conditions in the church at Colosse, he told of the presence of true Christian love among them. This was their love for one another, as mentioned earlier in 1:4. It was a demonstration that the Holy Spirit was active among them, producing the fruit which only He can do effectively (Gal. 5:22). This is the only explicit reference to the Holy Spirit in the epistle, although the word for Spirit is the root of the term "spiritual" (*pneumatikēi*) in 1:9. The ministry of the Spirit, however, is to glorify Christ (John 16:13-14), and this is the dominant feature of the epistle.

Something very important is revealed about the character of Epaphras in this brief reference. A lesser man would have been discouraged by the problems at Colosse. He might well have poured out to Paul his displeasure over the lack of discernment among some of the Christians who should have rejected these false teachers at once instead of continuing to give them a hearing. Yet Paul says that Epaphras had declared the good things about the believers, not the bad. He must have emphasized their love, not their failures. He was not in Rome as their accuser but as their minister, hoping to learn from the apostle how he could assist his congregation to be better. He knew that a good minister must follow the example of his Lord and expect not "to be ministered unto, but to minister" (Matt. 20:28).

Questions for Discussion

1. What are some ways in which Christians can display love to one another?
2. What is included in the believer's hope?
3. How does the Christian's hope inspire him to greater love and faith?
4. What are some of the names for the gospel in this passage? What aspects of the gospel do these names emphasize?
5. What characteristics of Epaphras made him an effective Christian worker?

3

Christ the Preeminent

COLOSSIANS 1:9-20

Most people are more concerned with action than with thought; practice is more popular than precept. Even Christians sometimes say, "Don't bother me with theology; all I want is a few guidelines on how to live." Yet Paul knew that genuine Christian conduct can be produced only when people are thinking correctly about Christian truth. And they will not understand Christian truth properly unless they have an accurate understanding of Jesus Christ—who He is and what He has done.

The apostle also knew the tendency of his readers to shy away from theological precepts unless these could be directly related to their daily lives. Therefore, Paul began his discussion by talking about what their lives should be like, and then went to the source from which Christian conduct flows.

I. EXPLANATION OF THE PERSON AND WORK OF CHRIST (1:9-29)

A. The Prayer Based on Christ (1:9-14)

1. The Occasion (1:9a)

VERSE 9. Paul voiced his understanding of the Colossians by a prayer to God to supply their needs. The phrase "since the day we heard it" looks back to the time when Epaphras had arrived in Rome with his report to Paul. Epaphras had told of their spiritual progress as well as the threat to their spiritual well-being. This information led Paul and Timothy to continual[1] prayer for the Colossian believers which pinpointed the true nature of their needs.

2. *The Petitions* (1:9b-12)

Two main petitions form the content of this prayer, the second growing out of the first and expanded by four coordinate Greek participles.

The first petition asked that the readers might have full knowledge of God's will. The term "full knowledge" (*epignōsin*) often carried a stronger force than "knowledge" (*gnōsin*), and denoted a more thorough understanding.[2] Later the Gnostics, a heretical group in Christendom, made much point of their *gnōsis*. It is tempting to think that Paul was opposing the early stages of that tendency here by implying that true Christian believers may possess an understanding of God's truth that is superior to any which a cultist could supply.

The knowledge which Paul desired for the Colossians was a knowledge of the will of God, which would operate in the sphere of spiritual wisdom and understanding. God's will has been revealed to mankind in the Word of God, and a thorough knowledge of it may be obtained through a careful and constant study of the Word as illuminated to the mind by the Holy Spirit. "Wisdom" (*sophiāi*) is the most general term covering the whole range of mental faculties. "Understanding" (*sunesei*) is more particular and special, referring to the application of wisdom to details. It brings the factors together and assesses the relation of things to each other. Hence a proper knowledge of God's will is not a mystical or esoteric experience, but involves the best use of one's intelligence.

The "wisdom" and "understanding" are both to be characterized as "spiritual," that is, operating in the realm controlled by the Holy Spirit. The Christian has a spiritual life which has

---

1. This unceasing prayer does not imply that Paul and Timothy were constantly voicing their prayer with no interruption whatever, but that they had not stopped their practice of prayer for the Colossians. In other words, the readers were still on their "active prayer list."

2. The respective verb forms of partial knowledge versus complete are contrasted by Paul in I Cor. 13:12, "Now I know in part (*ginōskō*), but then I shall know (*epignōsomai*). . . ." It is not insisted, however, that this rigid distinction is retained in all instances where the words are used separately.

been made alive by the Holy Spirit. Furthermore, the Spirit indwells each believer and should be in control of all his mental faculties. In addition, the Spirit inspired the Scripture which is God's revelation of knowledge (II Peter 1:21). Thus the full knowledge which believers should possess is "spiritual," for it is made available by the Spirit who inspired the Scripture and who illuminates its meaning for the earnest seeker.

VERSE 10. The second petition is a consequence of the first. The knowledge of God's will is desired for the believers so that they might walk in a manner worthy of the Lord. Proper conduct is the goal. The true knowledge of God always has practical effects. Of course, Paul does not mean that a believer's "walk" before God will make him "worthy" of salvation, for salvation is never earned (Eph. 2:8-9). Rather, he means that there is a Christian walk which is appropriate or suitable to his Christian profession. "Unto all pleasing" means "in all ways that are pleasing to God."

Paul gives four characteristics of this "worthy walk" which believers should display as they put into operation their growing knowledge of God's will. These characteristics are expressed grammatically by four Greek participles which are in a parallel construction. First, the believer who is walking properly before God will be "bearing fruit in every good work." "Fruit" is often used as a metaphor for "results" or "product" (Rom. 6:21-22). Paul used the term frequently to denote the various Christian characteristics which express the regenerated life within (e.g., Gal. 5:22-23). No limitation is indicated—every sort of good work is a legitimate opportunity for the Christian to put his new life into operation.

Of special interest is the slightly different form of the word for "bearing fruit" in 1:6 (a middle voice of the participle), compared to its use in 1:10 (an active voice[3]). In 1:6 the term is used of the gospel which "bears fruit of itself," that is, out of its own inherent energy (see comments on 1:6). In 1:10, however, the word describes believers, who do not bear fruit of themselves but by the power of the Holy Spirit. Thus a form of the word is used which does not suggest "of itself" or "of themselves."

The second characteristic of the worthy walk is "growing by

---

3. *karpophorountes* (active voice); *contra* the middle voice in 1:6.

the knowledge of God.'' Paul's figure of speech depicts a fruit tree which yields its fruit and keeps on growing, in contrast to grain which produces its harvest and then dies. As the fruit tree continues growing, it can yield even more fruit, and thus is a fine illustration of the believer, who should be demonstrating spiritual fruit in increasing quantity as his spiritual capacity enlarges through his growth in grace.

This spiritual growth occurs by the knowledge of God which the believer has acquired.[4] Paul has prayed that his readers might be filled with this knowledge (1:9). Now he voices his expectation that this knowledge would be used for producing growth.

VERSE 11. The third characteristic is ''being strengthened with all might.'' A similar statement in Ephesians 3:16 indicates that the source of this power is the Holy Spirit. Here is the enabling to walk in a worthy manner—it comes from the Spirit of God who works within the believer whenever he avails himself of this divine energy. How much power is available? It can be measured only in accord with ''the might of His glory'' (NASB margin). God's glories are the manifestations of His various attributes, one of which is omnipotence. Here then is the standard by which we can understand the sort of spiritual power available for us to live godly lives.

This strengthening, however, is not for the purpose of enabling believers to work great miracles or perform stupendous feats before a skeptical world. It is rather for the production of spiritual fruit, particularly under trying circumstances. The display of patience (endurance under trial) and longsuffering (non-retaliation), coupled with joy,[5] is not always easy to

---

4. This interpretation regards *tēi epignōsei* (the full knowledge) as a dative of means or instrument, a very common use of the dative when it occurs without a preposition. It avoids the awkwardness inherent in the common translation ''growing *in* the full knowledge of God,'' for Paul has prayed that they might be *filled with* the full knowledge in order to walk in a manner characterized by this growing. To grow *in* this knowledge would imply they were not yet filled with it.

5. I have placed ''with joy'' with the preceding words rather than with ''giving thanks'' as some advocate. Paul's other two uses of *eucharisteō* (give thanks) in this epistle (1:3; 3:17) do not utilize any reference to ''joy,'' indicating that joy may be implicit in thanksgiving without any additional reference. To place ''joy'' with ''patience'' makes good sense, and has a New Testament parallel in James 1:2-3.

demonstrate. But when the believer is confronted with adversity, whether from harsh circumstances or hostile persons, and can respond as Paul here describes, it is good evidence that he has learned something of the will of God, and has drawn upon the resources of the Holy Spirit.

VERSE 12. The fourth characteristic is "giving thanks." The Bible attaches great importance to this attitude, and regards unthankfulness as a mark of pagans and apostates (Rom. 1:21; II Tim. 3:1). This thanksgiving should be habitual with believers, and should involve a continuing recognition of what God has provided in salvation. It is He who has "qualified us" (NASB), not by any merits He saw in sinners, but by His gracious act of giving His Son whose perfect merits He has placed on the account of those who will trust Him for it.

This incomparable act of God has provided each believer with his share of the inheritance which has been reserved for the saints (see also 1:5). This inheritance is located "in the light," that is, in the realm which is the opposite of darkness (1:13). It is the realm where God is in perfect control (I John 1:5), a realm into which all believers have already been transferred in their spiritual lives, and from which they are to draw their power and their direction for their present Christian walk.

3. The Basis (1:13-14)

VERSE 13. Paul could pray such a prayer because believers stand in a special relation to God. First, they have been rescued from the realm of spiritual darkness (1:13a). The verb "rescued" (KJV, "delivered") suggests the danger of the situation. Sinful men are lost, unable to save themselves, and are dependent for rescue upon some source other than themselves. The rescuer of these lost people (here, Paul and the Colossians) was the Father (1:12), who intervened in their hopeless position and took them out from the realm of darkness. This "darkness" is the opposite of the "light" referred to in 1:12. It is that sphere of existence which is in opposition to God, and is characterized by sin (John 3:19; Rom. 12:12; I John 1:6; 2:11). The "authority" (KJV, "power") which the realm of darkness exercises refers to the jurisdiction of Satanic forces which keeps sinful men under the sway of the devil and his agents (Eph. 6:11-12).

Second, believers have been transferred into the kingdom of

God's Son (1:13b). The word "transferred"[6] (KJV, "translated") has been found describing the wholesale transportation of people following warfare.[7] Here it describes God's rescue of believers from the clutches of Satan's realm and their removal into the kingdom of Christ. Although the full establishment of this kingdom must await our Lord's return, believers have already been made citizens of it through regeneration (Eph. 2:19; Phil. 3:20), and presently enjoy some of its privileges. Paul's beautiful designation of this new dominion as "the kingdom of the Son of His love" was probably drawn from such statements of God to Jesus as "Thou art my beloved Son" (Luke 3:22).

VERSE 14. Third, believers possess redemption from sins. Because those who trust Christ for salvation are placed into a vital union with Him (note the phrase "in whom"), they possess the redemption from sin which His sacrificial death secured. "Redemption" (*apolutrōsis*) was a concept with which every reader, whether Gentile or Jew, was familiar. The Old Testament had taught its readers that life could be rescued by payment of a ransom (Exod. 21:30), and that sin could be atoned for by a sacrificed substitute (Lev. 4:1-21). Greek readers knew well the use of the term "redemption" in the practice of emancipating slaves by the payment of redemption-money.[8]

Lest there be any misunderstanding as to the nature of this redemption, Paul specified it as "the forgiveness of sins." Perhaps the false teachers at Colosse were using the term "redemption" in some other way. Surely they had misunderstood when they attributed some saving power to angels (2:18). By Christ's sacrifice of Himself at the cross,[9] He alone paid the redemption price that satisfied God's offended righteousness. As a result, the guilt and punishment which sin had incurred has been removed, and full redemption becomes the possession of those

---

6. Greek: *metestēsen.*

7. Josephus, *Jewish Antiquities* 9.11.1 (#235), trans. Ralph Marcus, in the Loeb Classical Library (Cambridge, 1937), VI, 124.

8. See Adolph Deissmann, *Light from the Ancient East* (Grand Rapids, reprinted 1965), pp. 318-30.

9. The words "through his blood" (KJV) do not appear in 1:14 in most ancient manuscripts. They were apparently added later, being drawn from the similar statement in Ephesians 1:7, where they properly belong.

Fig. 3. The mound of Colosse, view east. *Levant*

who are "in" Christ. Because the Colossian readers had been recipients of these incomparable gifts of God, Paul could pray for them as he did.

B. The Preeminence of Christ (1:15-20)

1. Christ the Image of God (1:15a)

VERSE 15. This section presents one of the great Christologies of the New Testament. Christ is described in three relationships. In relation to God He is the image (*eikōn*). Besides its general sense of "likeness," *eikōn* had a two-fold connotation.[10] First of all, it suggested *representation*. It did not connote accidental similarity, but a representation of something else, either from natural causes (as a child can bear the image of his father) or by design (a statue carved to be a famous man's image). To call Christ the image of God is to say that He represents God, and to

---

10. An excellent discussion of "image" is found in J. B. Lightfoot, *St. Paul's Epistles to the Colossians and to Philemon* (Grand Rapids, reprint edn.), pp. 143-46.

say that He "is" (*estin*) the image (rather than "became") shows that Paul is not speaking of the incarnation only, but of an eternal relationship. It is not the physical form of Jesus which is in view, but the very nature of God which Christ has always possessed.

But mankind also bears the image of God (see Gen. 1:26-27; I Cor. 11:7). Does this prevent us from thinking of the image which Christ had as a sharing of deity with the Father? A careful study of all relevant passages reveals a difference. Man is said to be *made* in the image of God. Thus he is a finite image, and subject to all the limitations of that plane of existence. Christ, however, *is* the image. He is the unoriginated, eternal, infinite image of God, on a far higher plane of existence. He not only shared certain God-like qualities as finite man does, but He is the image of God on the same eternal level as the Father Himself (John 1:1). Thus to call Christ the image of God is to identify Him with the eternal Logos, and to equate Him with God.

The second idea connoted by the term "image" is *manifestation*. Christ is "the image of the invisible God." This invisibility of God is not confined to physical sight, but to inward comprehension as well. The finite cannot comprehend the infinite, and thus we are dependent upon this divine image of God in order to know God. The same thought is expressed in many New Testament passages (Matt. 11:27; John 1:14, 18; 14:9; II Cor. 4:6).

2. *Christ Supreme over Creation* (1:15b-17)

"Firstborn of all creation" (NASB) describes Christ in relation to the natural creation. He is stated to be the Creator of all things and to occupy the position of "firstborn" (*prōtotokos*). A superficial reading of the phrase might suggest that Christ was a part of creation, even though He was the first to be created. Various heretical groups throughout Christian history have taught this.[11] However, the context clearly refutes this notion, for Christ is said to be the one who created *all* things (1:16, 17), not merely all *other* or all *subsequent* things.

The correct understanding of this passage treats the word "firstborn" in its common biblical sense of rank or sovereignty,

---

11. The Arian controversy of the fourth century is the most notable example, but modern cults such as Jehovah's Witnesses have perpetuated this heresy.

and regards the phrase "of all creation" as a comparative expression meaning "as compared to all creation."[12] Although "firstborn" can denote temporal priority (such as in Luke 2:7), thus affirming Christ's preexistence in relation to the created universe, it also conveys at times the idea of positional priority; this aspect is prominent here. An Old Testament illustration is found in the case of Jacob (Israel), the younger of Isaac's two sons, who was nevertheless elevated by God to a higher position than his older brother: "Israel is my son, even my firstborn" (Exod. 4:22). Eventually this term came to be used as a description of the Messiah, "I will make him my firstborn" (Ps. 89:27), depicting His sovereignty over all creation.

VERSE 16. This supremacy over creation is elaborated by five additional statements. First, Christ is the One in relation to whom all things were created. The phrase "in him" (*en autōi*) locates creative plans and forces as residing in Christ. This involves absolutely all of creation ("all things") in every locality ("that are in heaven and that are in earth"). It includes created things of every sort ("visible and invisible") and of every rank ("thrones or dominions or rulers or authorities," NASB).

The mention of the word "invisible" moved the discussion into the realm of spirit beings; Paul, therefore, listed a series of these angelic dignitaries.[13] In Gnostic systems and presumably at Colosse, angelic beings were graded into various ranks and varying amounts of worship were paid to each according to rank—to the neglect of Christ. Paul did not necessarily assert that such a gradation exists (although it may), and he certainly did not concur in a worship of angels. But he did indicate that Christ is the Creator of and thus superior to all angelic beings, regardless of how highly men may esteem them.

Second, Christ is the agent who created all things. "By him" (*di' autou*) indicates that creative force passed through Him into

---

12. The genitive of comparison is here influenced by the *prōto-* element of *prōtotokos*, and is similar to the genitive in John 1:15, *prōtos mou ēn* ("he was first as compared to me").

13. Additional references to angelic ranks appear in 2:10, and in Eph. 1:21, 3:10, and 6:12, making it clear that angels, not human dignitaries, are meant. The variety and lack of precise order in these lists is a caution against adopting too rigid a classification of angelic orders. Undoubtedly the angelic hosts are organized, but revelation is not detailed enough to warrant any complete description.

operation. The same phrase is used of Christ's creative function
by the apostle John (John 1:3). S. Lewis Johnson has described
Christ in this passage as both the architect ("in him") and the
builder ("by him") of creation.[14]

Third, Christ is the goal of all creation. All things have been
created "for him." The verb tense of "have been created" (perfect indicative, *ektistai*) points to the enduring condition of the
universe which "was created" in the past (aorist tense, *ektisthē*,
v. 16a). The phrase "for him" (*eis auton*) indicates that the
created universe is moving toward a goal; other Scriptures teach
that someday all opposing forces will be under Christ's feet and
He will be acknowledged as Lord of lords and King of kings
(I Cor. 15:25; Phil. 2:10-11; Rev. 19:16).

VERSE 17. Fourth, Christ is prior to all creation. He is "before
all things" (*pro pantōn*). His preexistence antedated all creation, and this statement clearly places Him outside of created
beings.

Fifth, Christ is the sustainer of all creation. "In Him all things
hold together" (NASB). The verb literally means "stand
together" or "put together."[15] The statement means that the
creation, which had its beginning by Christ's creative act, continues to exist because of Him. This thought is closely connected with the preceding emphasis, for Christ's preexistence is
a logical necessity if the sustaining of all created things depends
upon Him.

3. Christ the Head of the Church (1:18-20)

VERSE 18. As Christ is supreme over the natural creation, so
is He sovereign over the new creation, the church. Paul used the
illustration of the head and the body to depict this relationship.
In his earlier epistles he had written of the church as the body of
Christ (Rom. 12:5; I Cor. 12:12, 27), but the emphasis there had
been upon the unity with diversity which characterizes the
church. He had even spoken of the "ear" and the "eye" (parts

---

14. S. Lewis Johnson, Jr., "Christ Preeminent," *Bibliotheca Sacra*, Vol. 119,
No. 473 (January, 1962), pp. 14-15.
15. Greek *sunestēken*. See Wilhelm Kasch, "Sunistēmi," *Theological Dictionary of the New Testament*, ed. Gerhard Friedrich, trans. Geoffrey W.
Bromiley (Grand Rapids, 1971), VII, 896-98.

of the head) as representing individuals in the church (I Cor. 12:16-17, 21). In the Prison Epistles, however, the illustration is developed further.[16] Christ is pictured as the head of the church, supplying vital life and direction, and acting as its proper sovereign.

In His capacity as head of the church, Christ is the "beginning" (*archē*). The term points to source or origin, and can be understood in the sense of "beginner" (as in Rev. 3:14). Christ was not merely a teacher who inspired people by His instruction, for He is the church's source of life. This all came about by His death and resurrection whereby He is the "firstborn from the dead" (*prōtotokos ek tōn nekrōn*). The two-fold aspect of priority (in time and in rank) is doubtless to be understood here, just as in 1:15b. Christ's physical resurrection was the first true resurrection. He was the first in time to emerge from the realm of the dead with a glorified resurrection body, never to die again (I Cor. 15:20, 23).[17] However, by virtue of resurrection Christ has been elevated in rank to a position higher than any of the other resurrected dead will experience. He is seated at the Father's right hand (Acts 2:33 NASB; Phil. 2:9). Furthermore, it is Christ who will cause the resurrection of others (John 5:28-29; 6:40).

Christ, therefore, has "become" (*genētai*) preeminent in all things, in the new spiritual creation as well as in the first natural creation. He was always sovereign over the first creation by virtue of His absolute Being, but He had to "become" the firstborn with respect to the church. This He did by His incarnation, death, resurrection, and exaltation by the Father which followed (Phil. 2:5-9).

VERSE 19. Christ has preeminence over all things because all divine fullness dwells in Him. Although the term "Father" does not appear in the original text, the inference seems warranted that "God" or "the Father" should be understood as the subject of the verb. In the New Testament whenever this verb "to be pleased" is used of the Deity, the reference is always to God

---

16. The same advancement in the illustration is employed in Ephesians 1:22-23, 4:15-16, and 5:23.

17. It is assumed that the persons raised by Old Testament prophets or by Jesus and the apostles returned to mortal life and eventually died again.

the Father (Matt. 3:17; Luke 12:32; I Cor. 1:21; Gal. 1:15).[18] In
the eternal counsels of God, it was His good pleasure that the
fullness of deity should be shared by the eternal and divine Son,
and this divine pleasure in the Son was stated by the Father on
more than one occasion (Matt. 3:17; 17:5).

"Fullness" (*plērōma*) was a term used in Gnostic literature to
denote the totality of the divine powers and attributes. These
were considered to be distributed among various aeons or
emanations (i.e., actual beings who mediated between God and
men). The entire series of aeons was known as the *plērōma*.[19]
In Paul's day (a century before full-flowered Gnosticism), the
term apparently referred to the totality of the divine attributes,
as indicated by Paul's clarifying phrase in 2:9, "all the fulness
of Deity" (NASB).[20] Hence, in contrast to the heretical
teaching which would share divine honors with angelic beings
(2:18), Paul affirms that all the divine powers reside in Christ.
There are no other mediating agents. Furthermore, this fullness
which Christ possesses is a permanent possession (*katoikēsai*).
This verb "to dwell" differs from its synonyms by denoting a
permanent residence, not a temporary sojourn. There were
heretical groups in the first century (e.g., Cerinthian Gnostics),
just as there are today (Christian Science being one example),
which taught that divine powers resided only temporarily in
Jesus. Paul's statement labels all such ideas false.

VERSE 20. God's purpose in all these dealings with His creation was to "reconcile all things to himself." This purpose was
accomplished by the sending of Christ, whereby God "made
peace through the blood of his cross." Christ's death by
crucifixion was not martyrdom; it was a vicarious sacrifice which

---

18. It is grammatically possible to regard "all the fullness" as the subject of
"was pleased," but this involves an awkward personification in which
"fullness" is the reconciler and the peacemaker. Furthermore, the participle
eirēnopoiēsas (having made peace), which is governed by the subject of the
verb, is masculine, and thus could not properly depend upon the neuter
plērōma.

19. See the excellent excursus in J. B. Lightfoot, *Colossians and Philemon*,
pp. 257-73.

20. S. Lewis Johnson, however, argues that the "fullness" in 1:19 is "the
fullness of grace and power," a different use from that in 2:9. See his "From Enmity to Amity," *Bibliotheca Sacra*, Vol. 119, No. 474 (April, 1962), pp. 141-42.

satisfied God's righteous demands by paying in full the penalty for sin. The enmity which existed between God and a sinful universe has ceased because Christ's death made peace (Rom. 5:10, cf. 5:1). Only those who spurn Christ's offer in the gospel are still at war.

The New Testament doctrine of reconciliation is always viewed as a reconciliation made to God. "We were reconciled to God by the death of his Son" (Rom. 5:10). "All things are of God, who hath reconciled us to himself by Jesus Christ" (II Cor. 5:18). "God was in Christ, reconciling the world unto himself" (II Cor. 5:19). ". . . that he might reconcile both unto God in one body by the cross" (Eph. 2:16).

Paul also taught that the scope of this reconciliation involved "all things," including entities both on earth and in heaven. Yet Paul was clear in his teaching elsewhere that not everyone will be saved (Phil. 3:18-19). This problem is resolved by recognizing that reconciliation is not equivalent to salvation. Rather, reconciliation refers to the removal of the barrier between God and man through Christ's expiatory work so that God can deal with sinners in a new way.

Reconciliation, however, has both an objective and a subjective side. Objectively, from God's side, the barrier posed by sin has been removed by Christ's death, so that the way is open for sinners to come to Him. But reconciliation does not eliminate the need of individuals to respond in faith to this work of God. On the subjective side, men must accept the reconciliation which God has offered. This idea is clearly set forth in II Corinthians 5:18-21, where people whom God has reconciled (v. 18) are then urged to be reconciled to God (v. 20).

In what sense does reconciliation involve the created universe apart from humanity? Scripture teaches that the natural creation presently groans under God's curse, but that eventually the curse will be removed as a result of the perfect satisfaction which Christ's sacrifice made to God (Rom. 8:19-22). But why do things in heaven need this reconciliation? Scripture does not discuss this in detail, but a reasonable suggestion is that heaven was the setting of Satan's rebellion, and that even the angelic world is involved somehow in defilement (Job. 4:18; 15:15). In some way, therefore, Christ's death has dealt not only with the guilt but also with the defiling consequences of sin; even things in heaven have benefited from the Cross.

Christ stands supreme, therefore, over every conceivable entity except the Father Himself, and He is equal to the Father in every essential way because He is the very image of God. When Christians properly understand this incomparable person, no room is left for the sort of errors which cropped up at Colosse and which ever lurk to confuse the unwary.

Questions for Discussion

1. What are some outward signs of a person's growth in the knowledge of God?
2. In what ways is Christ the image of God?
3. What are the differences between the image of God in Christ and the image of God in men?
4. How many relationships which Christ bears to the natural creation can you name from this passage?
5. In what sense has God reconciled all things through Christ?

4

Christ the Reconciler

COLOSSIANS 1:21-29

Paul's theology was always practical. He was never content to revel in the great truths of God's operations in the universe without relating God's purposes to people. After explaining how God had devised the plan to make peace with a world by the blood of Christ, Paul related all of this to his readers by showing what significance it had for them. He then gave his testimony to show how he personally fit into God's program and what it meant in his life.

C. The Work of Christ (1:21-29)

1. *As Experienced by the Colossians* (1:21-23)

a. The need for Christ's work (1:21)

VERSE 21. In their pre-Christian state the Colossians had been "alienated" from God. The Greek term is derived from a word that meant "foreign or strange."[1] The Colossians were held under Satan's sway and had no vital relationship with God. They were also "hostile in mind" (NASB) toward God. Not only were they identified with another realm (that is, aliens), but they were also in active opposition to God. This hostility was centered in their thought life, and particularly in their spiritual and

---

1. The form in the text is *apēllotriōmenous*, related to the adjective *allotrios*, "what belongs to another," and is ultimately derived from *allos*, "another." (Friedrich Buchsel, "Allos," *et al.*, TDNT, I, 264-66.)

moral understanding.[2] Paul was not referring just to a few of the Colossians who were more flagrant violators of God's righteousness, but to *all* the Colossians. And, of course, every person comes under this charge. Every unbeliever has been affected in his thinking by sin and is hostile to God in various ways in his attitudes and thoughts.

Furthermore, the Colossians' alienation and hostility to God expressed itself in "evil deeds." They were sinners by practice, as well as in thought and nature. And what was true of the Colossians is also true of all other people, in our day as well as Paul's. "There is none righteous, no not one; there is none that understandeth; there is none that seeketh after God. They are all gone out of the way" (Rom. 3:10-12; cf. Ps. 14:1-3).

b. The nature of Christ's work (1:22a)

VERSE 22. Christ's work on the Colossians' behalf was to reconcile them to God. In contrast to their former state, Christ had "reconciled"[3] them to God by making peace through His death (see comments on 1:20). The barrier of a righteous standard that needed appeasement has been removed because Christ's sacrifice at Calvary fully satisfied God's demands. God can now deal with sinners in a different way because their guilt has been cared for. This was done, said Paul, "in the body of his flesh through death." The addition of the phrase "of his flesh" (*tēs sarkos*) emphasizes the fact of Christ's human, physical body, perhaps to avoid any possible confusion with the spiritual body, the church, mentioned in 1:18. It is also possible that Paul may have been counteracting a false teaching that denied the genuine physical body of Christ.[4]

c. The purpose of Christ's work (1:22b)

Christ's reconciling work occurred in order that believers

2. This moral dimension of the thought life is illustrated by the fact that the Septuagint translators used the word for "mind" (*dianoia*) as a frequent rendering for the Hebrew "heart" (*lēv*).

3. This exposition follows the aorist active reading *apokatēllaxen* ("he reconciled") as adopted by KJV, NASB, and NIV, rather than the passive form *apokatēllagēte* ("you were reconciled") found in some ancient manuscripts.

4. An early heresy known as Docetism explained the physical body of Christ as only an appearance, not as actual flesh, because of the mistaken idea that physical flesh is inherently evil.

might be appropriately presented (1:22b). It is difficult to trace the reference of the various pronouns in this section. Does "he" refer to God or to Christ? Does God present believers to Himself or to Christ? Or does Christ present them to Himself or to God? Grammatically there is no problem in regarding "him" (*autou*) as "himself." However, believers are described in Scripture as presented both to God (Rom. 14:10, Greek text) and to Christ (Eph. 5:27), and sometimes it is not clearly stated to whom the presentation is made (II Cor. 4:14). In view of the fact that Christ is God, it makes little practical difference. However, the grammatical connections of the sentence in its context suggest that God is the One who utilized Christ to reconcile all things to God. God did this through Christ's death on the cross so that believers could be presented to Christ at the judgment seat (Eph. 5:27).

A casual reading might suggest this to be a reference to the judicial aspects of the cross whereby believers have been given a perfect standing as "saints" before God. However, the conditional clause in 1:23 makes it clear that a future eschatological setting is in view. When Christ returns and believers stand before Him, His reconciling work will enable them to stand positionally as ones set apart (*hagious*, set apart, holy) from a condemned and sinful world, without defilement or blemish (*amōmous*, a term used of animals free from imperfection and hence acceptable as sacrifices), and not even accused of any fault (*anengklētous*). This last term denotes the effects of justification whereby Christ's merits are so perfectly applied to believers that judicially they are treated as if they had not sinned at all. Christ's reconciling work has removed the basis for condemnation.

d. The evidence of Christ's work (1:23)

VERSE 23. The evidence that Christ's reconciling work has been truly received by the one who claims to believe is his continuance in the faith. "If ye continue" states the test whereby one may examine himself to see whether he really has appropriated Christ's work on his behalf. To continue in the faith is to remain steadfast in one's commitment to Christ, without falling prey to the religious fads that periodically capture the attention of the church. One is not saved by his own efforts to please God; neither is he kept secure by human determination and perseverance. But the saved person *will* persevere because he has been made a new creation in Christ (II Cor. 5:17), and the new life implanted by Christ will be developed by the Spirit and brought to completion (Phil. 1:6). He whose "faith" does not continue with appropriate evidences reveals that he never had true saving faith at all (James 2:14, 17; I John 2:19).

Continuing in the faith meant to Paul far more than simply nominal affiliation with the Christians at Colosse. It involved, first of all, a proper foundation. Using the metaphor of a building, Paul indicated that an enduring faith must be correctly founded. The term employed here involved the basic idea of laying the foundation stones for a building.[5] In the Epistle to the Ephesians written at the same time, Paul used a similar description and referred to the foundation "of the apostles and prophets," that is, the correct doctrine taught by them, with Jesus Christ being the "chief corner stone" (Eph. 2:20). Only when one has heard the unadulterated gospel and has accepted its free offer of salvation through the sole merits of Jesus Christ the Savior does he have the proper foundation of Christian faith.

Furthermore, the Christian "superstructure" erected on this solid foundation should be firm and stable. The term *hedraioi* (KJV, "settled") denotes rigidity, and suggests the inward strength which believers should possess because they have been growing and have been made strong by the Holy Spirit (1:10-11). No lack of spiritual bracing should be evidenced in their Christian lives. No sagging or misalignment must mar the development of their Christian experience. Their "building" must be solid and strong.

Likewise there must be no shifting away from that hope provided them by the gospel (cf. 1:5). They must not only have inward stability of Christian character but also have a stability of position regarding their doctrinal foundation. Just as a tornado can blow a house from its foundations, so the persuasiveness of

---

5. Greek: *tethemeliōmenoi*, from *themelioō*. The perfect passive form denoted the present condition resulting from a previous action. In other words, the Colossians' present state should reflect their prior founding.

false teachers can threaten the careless and unwary. This process is continually occurring, and it is one of the means whereby God allows those who are not really a part of the church's life to be removed (I John 2:19). The true Christian, however, is characterized by his faithful adherence to the gospel which he has accepted.

This gospel was no isolated, exclusive little secret, dependent upon one's access to a select group of teachers at Colosse. It was rather the exciting message of God preached throughout the world by the energetic efforts of countless Christians. Literally the text says the gospel was proclaimed "in all creation which is under heaven." This does not mean, of course, that every individual on earth had already heard the gospel, but it does indicate the universality of the gospel (cf. 1:6), in contrast to the narrow extension of the Colossian heresy. The statement is a legitimate use of literary hyperbole, and should be regarded as a generalization not requiring statistical exactness. Yet it must not be overlooked that the gospel did spread with remarkable swiftness in the comparatively few years after Pentecost, and no one can state precisely just where its geographical limits were. It was regarding this gospel that the author was proud to say, "I Paul became a minister." He reveled in its truth and its transforming power. None of the difficulties of his ministry ever made him ashamed to acknowledge the privilege that was his.

2. As Ministered by Paul (1:24-29)

a. Paul's sufferings (1:24)

VERSE 24. The preceding clause served as a link to join this fuller discussion of Paul's ministry to the general theme. He immediately raised the question of his sufferings, because the reader might well wonder whether the gospel which Paul claimed to be supernatural was not somehow compromised if it could not protect its ministers from suffering. The apostle's answer was that he actually was rejoicing in his physical sufferings because he knew their real nature and their beneficial purpose. He was a prisoner in Rome as he wrote these words, and there had been many other sufferings throughout his apostolic career. Nevertheless he regarded these sufferings as literally "filling up the things lacking of the afflictions of Christ."

What did Paul mean by calling his sufferings the afflictions of Christ? Certainly he was not referring to Christ's expiatory sufferings which accomplished salvation for sinners. This term "afflictions" (*thlipseis*) is never used of those sufferings, and neither was there any lack to be filled by others. When Christ said on the cross, "It is finished," He meant exactly that (John 19:30). The notion that any saving merits can be provided by suffering saints in addition to Christ is surely foreign to Paul's thought.

Far better is the view that these sufferings are actually those which a hostile world imposed first upon Christ and continues to inflict upon those who are identified with Him. Jesus said this would happen (John 15:20). When Christ said to Paul on the Damascus road, "Why persecutest thou me?" (Acts 9:4), Paul had a direct indication that a believer's sufferings in the cause of the Lord are regarded by Christ as His own sufferings. Paul realized that his sufferings were not the result of a capricious

Fig. 4. Roman Forum in the city of Paul's imprisonment. *Levant*

fate, but that he was permitted to be identified with his Savior and enter into some of the same experiences Jesus had from an unbelieving world which still hated Him.

A second reason which made Paul's sufferings bearable was that he knew their purpose. They were incurred in his ministry on behalf of the body of Christ, the church.[6] He was a prisoner at that moment because of his efforts to extend the gospel and edify the churches. His sufferings were part of the price he was paying in order for the church, including those members at Colosse, to be more firmly established and expanded in the world.

b. Paul's message (1:25-27)

VERSE 25. Picking up the clause he used in 1:23, Paul enlarged the thought by explaining in more detail the character of his ministry. It was a ministry which was literally "in accord with the administration of God which was given to me." The term "administration" (KJV, "dispensation") originated from the concept of the management of a household (Greek: *oikonomia*), and is sometimes translated "stewardship." Paul was comparing his ministry to a responsibility in God's household, in which he was carrying out a task assigned to him by the owner.

His responsibility was intended as a benefit for the Colossians ("for you"), and consisted of fulfilling the word of God. "Fulfill" (KJV) here means to "carry out," and it involved the proclamation of God's truth in the gospel. This was Paul's commission, and he had devoted his life since his conversion to carrying out that stewardship entrusted to him.

VERSE 26. This message consisting of the Word of God is here described as a "mystery." In the Greek world the term was used in the plural to denote the secret rites of pagan cults which were revealed only to the initiates. Thus the ideas of secrecy and concealment were prominent in the concept. However, in the New Testament, this word is used in connection with "making known" or "speaking" the mystery (for example, I Cor. 2:7; 13:2; 15:51; Eph. 1:9; 3:3; 6:19). Furthermore, it is most unlikely

---

6. The explanatory clause makes it clear that the body referred to in 1:24 is not Christ's human body as in 1:22, but the spiritual body composed of true believers as in 1:18.

that Jesus' employment of the word was in any way colored by pagan Greek usage (Matt. 13:11; Mark 4:11; Luke 8:10). The Jews themselves were familiar with this term from their popular Greek Translation of the Old Testament (Dan. 2:19, 28, 29, LXX). As a theological term in the New Testament, the word denotes a revealed secret, a truth formerly not known to men but now revealed by God to His people.

This particular mystery had been hidden from[7] or since the ages of time long past and the generations which made up those ages, but now has been made clear to the saints, that is, to Christian believers.

VERSE 27. The seriousness of this revelation is indicated by the mention that God Himself intended for this mystery to be made known. The importance and value of the truth contained in it is expressed as "the riches of the glory of this mystery." When "glory" is used of God in the New Testament, it is a reference to the display of one or more of the divine attributes. Here the glory of this mystery is certainly the glory of God which is displayed in it. The great wealth of God's love, mercy, wisdom, and power is set forth in the truth which Paul here explains.

The mystery in view concerned particularly the Gentiles. One should consult the parallel passage in Ephesians 3:3-9 for Paul's further elaboration of the subject. Specifically, the mystery now made clear was this: "Christ in you, the hope of glory." The very essence of salvation is "Christ in you." An examination of the following passages makes this clear:

Rom. 8:10 (NASB)	"If Christ be in you . . . the spirit is alive"
II Cor. 13:5 (NASB)	"Jesus Christ is in you—unless indeed you fail the test"
Gal. 2:20	"Christ liveth in me"
Eph. 3:17	". . . that Christ may dwell in your hearts by faith"

---

7. The preposition *apo* ("from") is in contrast to *nun* ("now"), and is primarily temporal here, denoting the time in the past from which this condition had existed, rather than merely the persons *from whom* it had been hidden.

It is this fact of Christ dwelling in the heart of the individual believer in a vital, life-sharing union that provides "the hope of glory." Christ, the living hope (I Tim. 1:1), supplies the believer with his guarantee and assurance of future glory which is presently reserved for him in heaven (1:5).

Note the phrases "among the Gentiles" and "Christ in you" (i.e., "you Gentiles") in 1:27, and compare this passage with Ephesians 3:3-9 to understand fully what Paul was asserting. The mystery (that is, the revealed secret) was that Gentiles could be equal sharers of new life in Christ as fellow-members of the same spiritual body. The prospect of salvation for Gentiles was not new, for even the Old Testament expressed this thought (Isa. 49:6). The newly-revealed aspect was that Gentiles did not need to adopt Jewish rites and customs, but could be saved "as Gentiles" and still be "fellow-heirs, and of the same body, and partakers of his promise in Christ by the gospel" (Eph. 3:6). In Judaism opinion was settled that Gentiles could be saved only by becoming Jews. This idea persisted even in the early church among some of its Jewish members (Acts 10—11, 15).

c. Paul's purpose (1:28)

VERSE 28. It was the message regarding this Christ who offers salvation to Jew and Gentile alike that Paul and his associates were preaching. The word "preach" (*katangellomen*) which is used here carries the idea of a declaration of a completed happening, in distinction from its cognates and synonyms.[8] It emphasizes not so much the various aspects which compose the contents of Christian instruction as it does the announcement that certain things have been accomplished.

This declaration about the person of Christ and what He had accomplished did, of course, have its instructive elements, even though it was basically an announcement. It involved both warning (*nouthetountes*) and teaching (*didaskontes*). These are the negative and positive implications that are implicit in the proclamation of Christ and His gospel. "Warning" referred to the admonitions regarding sin, judgment, and the need for repentance. "Teaching" had to do with the positive instruction in

---

8. Julius Schneiwind, "Angelia, *et al*.," TDNT, I, 71-72.

Christian truth. Paul and his assistants never slighted the gospel message in order to be more popular or to gain more converts. They proclaimed the full story of Christ and did not ignore its implications. They did this, however, "with all wisdom." The phrase denotes the manner in which they proclaimed Christ, not the content of their preaching. They were not irrational fanatics but had an intelligent concern for appropriate methods that would be ethical and truthful, as well as effective. These elements in the preaching of Paul and Timothy should characterize all preaching, whether it be initial evangelism or further instruction in the faith.

The purpose of proclaiming the message of Christ was that Paul and Timothy might "present every man perfect in Christ." The term "perfect" (*teleion*) can be rendered "complete" or "mature." Although the term was used in contemporary mystery religions to denote members who were fully instructed (as opposed to the novices), there is no need to suggest that Paul borrowed the term from that source, for Jesus also used it (Matt. 5:48). This perfection or completeness is stated as "in Christ." Every believer is judicially perfect the moment he is saved because of his identification with Christ (2:10). There is also a personal maturity which believers can progressively develop as they grow in their spiritual understanding and become more like Christ. A level of relative maturity is attainable in this life (James 1:4; I Cor. 2:6; Eph. 4:13-14). In this passage, however, it is likely that Paul was speaking about the end of the process. The statement "that we may present" suggests the occasion to be Christ's return, when all earthly ministries will be finished and each believer will be evaluated by his Lord (cf. Eph. 5:27).

The emphasis upon the universality of the gospel message, indicated by the three mentions of "every man" in this verse, may be a pointed contrast to the exclusivists in the Lycus Valley. They had no message for every man but only a human philosophy for those who shared their special "knowledge."

d. Paul's power (1:29)

VERSE 29. To accomplish the great purpose of making Christ's work known to men and then to bring those men to spiritual maturity is no easy task. The development of Christian growth among new converts is always a difficult and often a discouraging struggle. All sorts of opposition must be faced and overcome if one is to succeed. No less an expert than the apostle Paul had to "labor" (*kopiō*, a term denoting wearisome toil), expending great energy—physical, mental, and spiritual. A reading of his activities in the book of Acts, or a study of his experiences listed in II Corinthians 11:16-33, gives some indication of his toils in pursuing his task. Not the least of the difficulties encountered is the frequent need to be "striving" or contending with adversaries (*agōnizomenos*, a common athletic metaphor depicting the struggle against an opponent). There is always the world, the flesh, and the devil to be faced as one endeavors to encourage the program of God in a world that is hostile to God.

But Paul was not limited to his own human resources for the power to succeed. Rather, he labored in accord with Christ's "working which worketh in me mightily." The Greek term *energeian* ("working") is the source of the English word "energy." In the New Testament it was used only by Paul, and he employed it always when speaking of superhuman power. Six times[9] it described the power of God in operation, and twice[10] it referred to Satan's power. It always denoted effective power, power which was able to accomplish whatever task it undertook. Thus Paul says he could rely upon the power of God which was always sufficient for the work to be done, and which was at the moment of writing[11] putting forth its energy "in power"[12] (*en dunamei*; KJV, "mightily"). The fact that God was working in Paul, however, did not lessen the apostle's need to involve himself strenuously in his gospel labors. It merely meant that his labors and struggles would not be futile because God was empowering him. The message of Christ the Reconciler would succeed because God Himself supplied the power to sustain His messengers.

---

9. Eph. 1:19; 3:7; 4:16; Phil. 3:21; Col. 1:19; 2:12.
10. II Thess. 2:9, 11.
11. Indicated by the present participle *energoumenēn*.
12. The term *dunamis* is sometimes used to denote a miracle. However, a reference to God's power as working miracles through Paul would have been better expressed with a plural. Furthermore, mention of a miracle would be out of place in a context referring to Paul's wearisome toil and continual struggling.

Questions for Discussion

1. How did Christ's death reconcile us to God?
2. What are some evidences that a person has genuinely received Christ's reconciling work?
3. What was the mystery which God revealed in Colossians 1:21-29?
4. What should be the goal of preaching?
6. What are the characteristics of the person who is spiritually mature?
6. If God was working mightily in Paul, why did Paul need to labor and strive?

5

The Apostle's Concern

COLOSSIANS 2:1-5

There are many people who carry out life's duties without a real commitment. They do what is required, but very little else. A smaller number fulfill their own tasks with genuine dedication; their zeal knows no bounds when their own interests are involved. These are the ones who often rise rapidly in their chosen fields. But in devoting all their interest and efforts to the task at hand, they have little time or concern for anything which does not pertain directly to their own enterprise. Occasionally, however, one encounters a person whose dedication to a cause is so deep that it transcends his own narrow segment, and grasps the importance of the whole.

The apostle Paul was one of these. His commitment to Christ and His church was so statesman-like that he felt deeply concerned about the affairs of churches, even when the people were largely strangers to him, and when others were more immediately responsible for their care. Such an instance is seen in the present passage, where Paul revealed the depth of his interest in these readers, even though he had not known most of them personally. He had a concern for the whole church, not just for those Christians who happened to be near him at the time. He knew the reality of the oneness in Christ which all believers share, and he felt constrained to help Christians everywhere to grow in their spiritual lives and to stand firm against the evils of religious falsehood.

II. WARNING AGAINST THE PHILOSOPHIES OF MEN (2:1-23)

A. Paul's Personal Concern (2:1-5)

1. The Nature of Paul's Concern (2:1a)

VERSE 1a. The term "conflict"[1] (KJV) or "struggle" (NASB) points to an intense strain. The word is related to the term "striving"[2] in 1:29, and doubtless continues the athletic metaphor of a contestant expending great energy in his struggle to win the victory against formidable opponents. Some of Paul's struggles on behalf of the churches involved such difficulties as the hardships of travel, suffering in persecution, and hostility

Fig. 5. Greek vase painting of boxers in athletic struggle. Paul used this metaphor in 2:1 and 4:12. *The Metropolitan Museum of Art*, Rogers Fund, 1906.

---

1. Greek: *agōna.*
2. Greek: *agōnizomenos.*

from teachers of error. But there were inward struggles as well. A cognate of this word occurs in 4:12, where the expression "laboring fervently in prayers"[3] shows that conflict can also be a spiritual concern for the welfare of the believers. In 2:1, this kind of struggle is probably in view since Paul was at that time experiencing house arrest. He was not struggling against physical obstacles but against anxieties and deep concerns which he felt over the dangerous doctrines being promoted at Colosse and Laodicea. By letting his readers know of his strong concern, Paul conveyed to them the seriousness of their situation.

2. The Objects of Paul's Concern (2:1b)

VERSE 1b. Paul's first concern was the Colossians ("you"). The letter was addressed to them (1:2), and it was their minister Epaphras who had come from Colosse to Paul. Presumably it was this church in which the chief danger existed. (See chapter 1, "Introduction," for a description of the city.)

The apostle was also concerned for the Christians in Laodicea, a neighboring city ten miles to the west of Colosse. Laodicea was located on the same highway from Ephesus which also passed through Colosse. It was famous for the production of woolen garments and carpets made from the black wool of sheep raised on her grazing lands. The prosperity and importance of the city was attested in the writings of Strabo[4] and Tacitus.[5] It was also reflected in the letter to the Laodicean church included in the Book of Revelation by the apostle John (Rev. 3:14-22). Apparently the same doctrinal errors were being promoted at Laodicea, and therefore Paul wanted the Laodiceans to read this Colossian epistle and profit from the same warnings. There was also evidently another letter from Paul which was sent directly to the Laodiceans (4:16).

Paul concluded his mention of the objects of his concern by referring to "as many as have not seen my face in the flesh." It is conceivable that these words could designate a different group from the Colossians and Laodiceans. This would thus imply that the previously named groups *had* seen Paul personally. How-

---

3. Greek: *agōnizomenos . . . en tais proseuchais.*
4. Strabo, *The Geography* XII, 578 (12.8.16).
5. Tacitus, *The Annals* XIV.27.

Fig. 6. Ruins at Laodicea, a few miles from Colosse in the Lycus Valley. *Levant*

ever, there are clear instances where "and as many as"[6] names the whole class of which the ones previously mentioned were a part. Acts 4:6 and Revelation 18:17 are two clear examples of this usage. Furthermore, the mention of "their hearts" in 2:2 is obviously referring to the "as many as" of 2:1, and yet the Colossians are clearly a part of the reference as indicated by the term "you" in 2:4. Hence it is logical to infer that Paul is broadening his reference to include not only the Colossians and Laodiceans but also all the others in that vicinity who were likewise facing this threat to their faith. They may not have known Paul personally because he had not founded these churches (see chapter 1, "Introduction"), but they could be

6. Greek: *kai hosoi.*

assured that if they were part of the church of Jesus Christ, Paul had a deep concern for their welfare.

3. The Purpose of Paul's Concern (2:2-3)

a. The general purpose (2:2a)

VERSE 2a. Paul wanted his readers to be encouraged. The word "comfort"[7] had a wider meaning in the days of the KJV translators than at present. The idea in this context is not so much that of consoling the grief-stricken, but of encouraging, confirming, or strengthening the perplexed. The apostle was not trying to comfort his readers because of the damage which false teaching may have done in their midst, but rather to encourage them to stand firm and to press toward the goal of full understanding, which he mentions next.

In Paul's thought, as in the rest of Scripture, the "heart" symbolized much more than just the feelings or emotions of a person. It was a metaphor for the inner man, in which the mind has a vital part. According to the Bible, a man thinks with his heart (Prov. 23:7). Thus Paul wanted the believers' understanding regarding the person of Christ to be strengthened so that they would not be led astray.

b. The specific purposes (2:2b-3)

VERSE 2b. The general statement in which Paul expressed his desire for his readers was further expanded as he named several specific matters which would produce the encouragement he sought for them. First, spiritual encouragement would be theirs when they were "knit together in love." The presence of un-Christian teaching in a church is always divisive. Unity is quickly lost, and the loving concern for the best interests of one another which should characterize believers soon disappears. Paul knew that if the Christians in Colosse would stop lending a sympathetic ear to the smooth-talking errorists, and would join in an even closer union of hearts, it would do much toward providing the strength and encouragement vital to spiritual victory in an hour of crisis.

Second, this union of hearts in love was not an end in itself,

---

7. Greek: *paraklēthōsin.*

but was directed toward ("unto") the goal of acquiring full assurance of understanding. As long as the believers were uncertain about the basic truths of their faith they were vulnerable, able to be swayed by any persuasive teacher who might appear. Their "understanding"[8] was their ability to bring together the various data and concepts which related to the subject under discussion, and put them together in the proper way. Presumably the Colossians had been taught accurately by Epaphras and perhaps others. Their understanding should have been correct. Now what was needed was the "full assurance" that their understanding was true. When such confidence was achieved, based upon a proper understanding of God's truth, the readers would be in possession of a great treasure. Paul called it the "riches of the full assurance of understanding." Spiritual prosperity consists of understanding God's truth and being confident of it. Too many of God's people live lives of spiritual poverty, uncertain of what God has provided for them, and become easy prey for every cult and religious charlatan that comes along.

A third phrase provides further explanation of this understanding which Paul wants the readers to have, and should probably be regarded as parallel to the preceding thought. If the Colossians were to stand firm against the enticing doctrines that were being presented to them, they needed a full knowledge[9] of the "mystery of God." That is, their understanding had to be thorough and assuring regarding the truth which has been revealed to men in the Word of God. Paul had already referred to the "mystery" as truth previously unknown but now revealed by God to those who would receive His Word (1:26).

A great many textual variants occur at the end of 2:2, but the preferred texts read this way: "the mystery of God, [namely] Christ."[10] By putting "Christ" in apposition with "mystery," Paul has stated that the very essence of God's revelation to mankind is the person of Christ. It is He who has revealed God to men ("the image of the invisible God," 1:15), and who has

---

8. Greek: *tēs suneseōs*.

9. Greek: *epignōsin*.

10. This reading, *tou mustēriou tou theou, Christou*, is supported by P[46] and B, and is adopted by UBS and Nestla-Aland.

reconciled men to God (1:20-22). Thus the more that Christians understand of the person and work of Christ, the more able they are to recognize and refute religious error that is often superficially attractive.

VERSE 3. The reason why it is so vitally important for Christians to have a proper knowledge of Christ is because in Him are hid "all the treasures of wisdom and knowledge." All that a person needs to know in order to establish an eternal relationship with God can be found in Christ and His accomplishment for mankind. "Knowledge" denotes the apprehension of truths. "Wisdom" is more general and connotes an understanding of the relations among the various truths, and the application of them to specific situations. Were the Colossian teachers insisting that they had a monopoly on some religious truth? Did they suggest that trusting Christ was not enough to bring salvation? They certainly implied that Christ alone was not sufficient by insisting upon the need to worship angels (2:18). Did they demand that Mosaic regulations must still be observed, even though Christ had indicated otherwise (2:16)? Paul let his readers know that in Christ are *all* the treasures that will make a person knowledgeable and wise regarding life with God. These are treasures of inestimable value, and they are *all* to be found in Him.

We should not miss, however, the implication of the term "hid." The word means concealed, stored up, or hidden. The thought is that if we possess Christ (and every believer does, John 14:23), then we possess all the treasures. But inasmuch as the treasures are hidden in Christ, believers must grow in their understanding of Christ in order to enjoy the treasures. Even the newest believer is "in Christ" and Christ is in him, but there must be a growth "in grace and in the knowledge of our Lord and Savior Jesus Christ" (II Peter 3:18). Not all believers are equally aware of the riches they possess in Christ. Here then is a challenge to the Colossians and to us to search deeply into the Word of God to discover the treasures that are ours in Him.

4. The Cause of Paul's Concern (2:4-5)

a. The presence of deceitful teachers (2:4)

VERSE 4. "This I say" has reference to the preceding, 2:1-3, in which Paul has mentioned his extreme concern for the

Colossians and their Christian neighbors. He has listed the goals which he wanted them to reach. Next he proceeds to explain the reasons why he was so concerned. Two factors were particularly relevant.

The first factor was the presence of deceitful teachers in the Colossians' midst. These teachers majored in persuasive speech (KJV, "enticing words"). In classical Greek the term (*pithanologia*) did not have a negative connotation. It denoted probable reasoning as opposed to demonstration.[11] Whatever bad implications it may have in this context are drawn from the word "beguile" (*paralogizētai*). Treating the term as a neutral one, the reader can conclude that these dangerous teachers were extremely eloquent and persuasive. Truth itself can be persuasive, but when truth has been abandoned or distorted by a teacher, he must depend for his effectiveness upon such tactics as oratory. Christian history is filled with smooth-talking charlatans. It matters not whether their platform is a pulpit or a classroom, a radio microphone, or a television camera. Eloquence and persuasiveness can be a great asset in the proclamation of truth, but it can also mask serious error. The discerning listener must evaluate what he hears and must test it by the Word of God.

Paul feared that his readers might be deceived by the sheer eloquence of some unscrupulous religious promoters. "Beguile" is the translation of a term which means to reason falsely, to deceive, or to cheat by a false reckoning. When men learn the power of skillfully-used words, they sometimes sacrifice their integrity and use their skill for selfish interests. It must be assumed that much of the problem at Colosse was caused by persons who either did not understand true Christian doctrine or else willfully perverted it, and then used their skillful rhetoric to promote their own religious schemes.

Paul asserted that this disastrous development was not to be tolerated in even one instance ("lest any man"). Paul's statement did not mean that one problem teacher was causing all the

---

11. H. G. Liddell, and R. Scott, rev. H. S. Jones, *A Greek-English Lexicon* (Oxford, n.d.), II, 1403; T. K. Abbott, *Epistles to the Ephesians and to the Colossians* in the International Critical Commentary series (Edinburgh, reprinted 1974), p. 242.

trouble at Colosse. What was meant was that not even one such person should be given any opportunity to divert God's people from the truth which they had been taught.

Paul's warning should be heeded just as carefully by today's Christians, for the danger continues to plague believers, and the same persuasive tactics still trap the unwary. The colorful brochure, the polished "sales pitch," the skillful use of mass communications media, and the employment of every psychological gimmick known to man are thrown into the battle to win the religious interest of the unsuspecting. The danger in Paul's day caused him deep anguish and concern (2:1). The threat today is surely no less.

b. The absence of Paul (2:5)

VERSE 5. The second factor which caused Paul's concern was his inability to be present at Colosse and to take a personal hand in refuting the error that was threatening the church. To one who was as energetic and skillful in argument as was Paul, the forced confinement which had already lasted about four years must have been galling to his active spirit. How he would have liked to withstand these adversaries to the face, and at the same time use his boundless energies and devotion to build up the believers in their faith! But physically ("in the flesh") he was prevented from following that course. Two years had been spent in a prison at Caesarea (Acts 24:27); another fall and winter had seen him transported as a prisoner to Rome (Acts 28:11); now nearly two more years had elapsed in which he was confined in Rome (Acts 28:30). No one could fault him for his absence from Colosse, for it had been beyond his control. Yet he was deeply conscious of the fact that his absence complicated his dealing with the problem.

While conceding[12] that he must be physically absent, Paul quickly added that he was not cut off from his interest in these readers. The phrase "I am with you in spirit" indicated that his concern and prayers continued to bring him and the Colossians

---

12. *Ei kai* introduces here a clause of logical concession, and should be rendered "even though." H. E. Dana, and J. R. Mantey, *A Manual Grammar of the Greek New Testament* (New York, 1946), p. 292; W. F. Arndt and F. W. Gingrich, *A Greek-English Lexicon of the New Testament* (Chicago, 1957), p. 219.

into each other's presence, so to speak. The reference here is to Paul's own spirit, not the Holy Spirit; this is made clear by the obvious contrast to "the flesh" which refers to Paul's bodily presence. Of course, the Christian's spirit should always be controlled by the Holy Spirit, and in this instance with Paul it undoubtedly was.

Furthermore, the report he had received from Epaphras (1:8) had enabled him to be very much aware of the Colossians' situation. The message was not all gloom and pessimism. To be sure there was trouble at Colosse, but there was victory too. Consequently the message had caused him to rejoice over their faith, and this in turn led him to see in his mind's eye the steadfastness of their trust in Christ.

The term translated "order" (KJV) or "ordered array" (NASB margin) was often used as a military term (*taxin*), perhaps suggested by the presence of the praetorian guard at this time of Paul's imprisonment. The word described the orderly line of soldiers, without ragged sections or breaks. The second term, "steadfastness" (KJV) or "stability" (NASB), comes from a word which is used to describe something as firm, stiff, strong, or solid (*stereōma*). It can depict a castle or bulwark.[13] In the present context it describes the collective aspect of the Colossians' faith. Each believer was still in his place (*taxin*) and collectively the church was maintaining a solid front (*stereōma*) against the foe. No one had broken ranks or defected; the church was not tottering. The apostle's concern was that this steadfastness of faith would continue, and that the adversaries would at length be silenced. Paul could not instruct the Colossian church in person, but the epistle he was sending would be a worthy substitute. And it would have one additional advantage: it could be used by other churches when they too faced such a problem. Nineteen centuries later it is still a formidable weapon.

Questions for Discussion

1. What does Colossians 2:1 indicate about Paul's personal relations with the Colossians?
2. What is the "mystery of God"?

---

13. Georg Bertram, "Stereos, *et al.*," TDNT, VII, 614.

3. If all wisdom and knowledge are in Christ, why should a Christian study?
4. What are the best safeguards against the persuasive speech of false religious teachers?
5. In what ways can one Christian be with another "in spirit"?

6

The Centrality of Christ

COLOSSIANS 2:6-15

The importance of Christ in men's religious thinking is widely acknowledged. Even groups which do not call themselves Christian often regard Jesus Christ as one of the foremost of the world's spiritual leaders. His ethical precepts, His remarkable life, and the impact which His brief time on earth has made upon history are generally admired.

The problem comes, however, when one confronts the precise claims which the Bible makes for Christ. He is not set forth as merely another religious figure. He is not presented as simply a visionary man who was misunderstood, and from whom moral lessons can be learned. On the contrary, when Jesus Christ is viewed from the biblical perspective, He is shown to be uniquely divine, and the One who alone can provide salvation for men—not by His moral teachings but by His sacrificial death and subsequent resurrection. It is this view of Christ in which the heresy at Colosse fell short, and which many a cult since has denied. Christ is central to true Christian faith, and that point is clearly explained in this section of Paul's letter.

B. The True Doctrine of Christ (2:6-15)

1. *The Encouragement toward True Doctrine* (2:6-7)

a. Past experience recalled (2:6a)

VERSE 6a. "As ye have received Christ Jesus the Lord"

---

1. Greek: *paralabete*.

reminds the readers of their previous experience when they had responded to the gospel. "Received"[1] is the common word for receiving instruction from teachers. It has particular reference here to the instruction received by the Colossians from their properly qualified teachers. Other New Testament passages which utilize the term in this way are I Corinthians 15:1, 3; Galatians 1:9; Philippians 4:9; I Thessalonians 2:13, 4:1; and II Thessalonians 3:6. These first readers had been instructed by Epaphras (1:7) and perhaps others. Paul explained that they were not to waver in the face of instruction that contradicted what they had been taught.

"As" should be understood to indicate the manner in which their Christian lives were to proceed. They were to be living *as* they had been taught. Their conduct and faith was to be in accordance with the teaching they had received.[2] The context emphasizes this (2:7, "as ye have been taught"), and is clearly a response to the false teaching which threatened them.

To be specific, it was "Christ Jesus the Lord" who had been taught to them. The rather unusual use of the article in this expression[3] suggests that the translation should be "the Messiah, Jesus the Lord"[4]; this identifies precisely who this Messiah is. It also counteracts two false impressions, for it recognizes the historical person Jesus (in contrast to Docetism, which denied His genuine humanity), and acknowledges Him as the Lord (in contrast to the lower view promoted at Colosse).

b. Present duty exhorted (2:6b-7)

VERSE 6b. "Keep walking in Him" is a good way to understand the present tense of the imperative verb used here. The progressive conduct of the Colossians' Christian life was to correspond to the teaching which they had received. "In Him"

---

2. Another interpretation views the statement to mean that just as the Colossians had received Christ by faith, so they should continue walking by faith. However, the limitation of the reference to faith does not seem to be the only point of the passage. The insistence rather is upon the need to walk in harmony with all that they had been taught (2:6, 7).

3. Greek: *ton Christon Iēsoun ton kurion.*

4. J. B. Lightfoot, *St. Paul's Epistles to the Colossians and to Philemon* (Grand Rapids, reprinted), p. 176; T. K. Abbott, *A Critical and Exegetical Commentary on the Epistles to the Ephesians and to the Colossians* in the International Critical Commentary series (Edinburgh, reprintd 1974), p. 244.

denotes the fact that believers are sharers of Christ's life. They are in Him and He is in them (John 14:23; 15:3, 5; 17:23), and this spiritual reality should be reflected in the lives they live.

VERSE 7. The kind of walk that properly displays the Christian instruction will reveal itself in four ways. Paul conveyed the thought by using four participles that are grammatically parallel. The first is, "having been firmly rooted" (NASB). It is a perfect passive tense form, depicting the present condition resultant from a past action. At the Colossians' conversion, God had planted them firmly in the Christian faith, and the roots of their faith had continued ever since. This, of course, is basic to any Christian living. The Christian life is not merely a lifestyle to be assumed or discarded as interests rise or wane. Rather, it is a life that depends upon a new birth.

The second characteristic of a proper walk in Him is "being built up in Him." This is a present participle, as are the next two, and it stresses the continuing activity which is expected. The word suggests the process of building in successive layers,[5] and reminds us that the Christian life is not a swift accomplishment but a lifelong process. The passive voice, "being built up,"[6] indicates that the believer is dependent upon God to make this possible. Believers are responsible to use the spiritual nourishment provided in the Word (I Peter 2:2) and to follow its wholesome commands for living (I Tim. 6:3) in order that spiritual growth may take place, but it takes God Himself to produce growth in His children.

"Being established in the faith" is the third characteristic. It describes the believer as becoming increasingly stable and firm in his spiritual life. On the assumption that "the faith" here refers to the body of Christian doctrine[7] (i.e., the Christian faith), Paul was doubtless thinking particularly of his readers' need to withstand any shakiness in the presence of false doc-

---

5. J. B. Lightfoot, *Colossians*, p. 177.

6. Greek: *epoikodomoumenoi*.

7. There is some manuscript evidence for omitting "in" (*en*), and thus the expression could be treated as a dative of means, "by means of your faith." However, even if this omission be preferred, the dative is more likely showing reference or respect, so that the idea is the same as given in the exposition: "established with respect to the faith."

trine. It was imperative that they have a growing conviction of the truth they had received.

The fourth phrase in the series, "abounding with thanksgiving," echoes a theme that was prominent in Paul's writings (e.g., 1:12; 3:15, 17; I Thess. 5:18). The apostle knew well that a proper understanding of what God had provided believers in Christ would inevitably result in thanksgiving. And a thankful spirit is not a fretful spirit which lays itself open to doubts or to wrong ideas about what God has done.

2. *The Danger to True Doctrine* (2:8)

a. The capture attempted (2:8a)

VERSE 8a. The warning "beware lest" (KJV) or "see to it" (NASB) awakens the reader to the existing danger, which the author regarded as very real.[8] The danger was that someone might capture the Colossians with his false teaching, just as vicious men might kidnap a defenseless victim. The word *sulagōgōn*, translated "spoil" (KJV) or "take captive" (NASB), occurs only here in the New Testament, and not in any earlier Greek writer. Its components (*sulē* and *agō*) mean "to carry away booty." Hence the interpreter must decide whether the word is to be understood here as "rob" (i.e., take a spoil or booty from someone) or "to capture." In favor of the latter sense is the fact that the direct object of the verb is stated as "you." Furthermore, if the meaning were "rob," then one would expect the text to state what was stolen, and yet it never does. Much better is the thought that Paul meant the Colossians themselves to be in danger of capture. If the false teachers could enlist these believers under their banner, they would not have merely robbed them of certain truths, but would have captured their allegiance.

---

8. The contruction *blepete mē* usually takes the subjunctive in the New Testament (Matt. 24:4; Mark 13:5; Luke 21:8; Acts 13:40; I Cor. 8:9; 10:12; Gal. 5:15; Heb. 12:25), but here it is followed by the future indicative *estai*. The difference may emphasize that the danger is viewed as real, not merely a hypothetical possibility. See Lightfoot, *Colossians*, p. 178; Abbott, *Colossians*, p. 246; J. H. Moulton, *A Grammar of New Testament Greek*, Vol. I, *Prolegomena* (Edinburgh, 1908), p. 178.

b. The method employed (2:8b)

VERSE 8b. First, the possible capture of the Colossians would not be by physical violence but "through philosophy and empty deception" (NASB). In Paul's day the term "philosophy" was used variously, but one clear illustration of its usage in Jewish circles was its employment by Josephus to describe the Jewish religious-political parties—the Pharisees, Sadducees, and Essenes.[9] Discussions about God and the world and the meaning of human life could also be described by this term. Paul was not deploring all study of this sort. Properly defined, Paul himself was an outstanding expounder of true philosophy. He possessed divine revelation as to how God, the world, and human life should truly be understood. What he was deploring here was *tēs philosophias* ("his[10] philosophy"), that is, the speculations of the teachers at Colosse. Philosophy's value is in direct proportion to its adherence to truth. When it is mere "philosophizing" out of sin-distorted reasoning, it offers no help but is only empty deception. The philosophy Paul was describing may have hidden its barrenness under beautiful and persuasive oratory (2:4), but it was deceiving for it proclaimed itself as truth when in reality it was error.

Second, this false doctrine was "according to the tradition of men." "Tradition" means that which is handed down as instruction, whether orally or in writing. The term does not necessarily denote secrecy or variance from the truth, for sometimes it is used of Christian instruction given by the apostles (II Thess. 2:15; 3:6). In Colosse, however, the religious philosophy being promoted was a tradition that was purely human. It had no supernatural source, and was merely human speculation. It may have sounded pious, using references to angels (2:18) and employing Old Testament ceremonies (2:16), but the way these things were put together and the conclusions drawn from them were totally false.

Third, this teaching was also in accord with "the elementary principles of the world" (NASB). The expression in the original

---

9. Josephus, *Antiquities of the Jews* 18.1.2 (18:11).

10. The article with *philosophias* particularizes the "philosophy" and is best expressed in English as a pronoun.

text is a difficult one because the Greek word *stoicheion* has a variety of meanings. Basically it denotes that which belongs to a series,[11] and was applied to such things as the syllables which make up a word, the elements which make up the cosmos, and the notes in a line of music. In Hebrews 5:12 the sense of the word is "first principles," that is, the basic elements of instruction in the Word of God.

In Colossians it is apparent that *ta stoicheia*[12] refers to some kind of teaching. It was part of the philosophy which was being advanced with persuasive speech (2:4), and was a teaching which was contrary to what the Colossians had been taught by their original Christian instructors (2:7). Comparison with the same expression in Galatians 4:3 and 4:9 sheds more light on Paul's thought. There Paul wrote about Jewish ceremonies connected with the Mosaic law. Before the Christian faith had come, Jewish people were held in bondage under such regulations, and Paul called them "the elemental things of the world" (4:13 NASB).[13] When the Galatian Christians were tempted to revert to such practices, the apostle termed it a return to the "weak and worthless elemental things" (4:9 NASB).[14]

Hence it is best to regard "the elementary principles of the world" as referring in this passage to the religious practices, particularly ceremonial observances, which the false teachers were promoting. Many of these practices were derived from the Old Testament system (compare 2:16), but they were now being misunderstood and misapplied. They were "of the world" in the sense that they dealt with physical and material matters which were only temporary shadows of the reality provided in Christ (2:17). Even the worship of angels (2:18) could have been related to this insistence upon observing the Jewish law inasmuch as angels were viewed as God's instruments in giving the law to Israel (Acts 7:53; Gal. 3:19; Heb. 2:2).

Finally, to state it negatively, this teaching was not "according to Christ." He was not its source nor its content. It

---

11. Gerhard Delling, "Stoicheion," TDNT, VII, 670.
12. In Col. 2:8 and 2:20 the plural form is used.
13. Greek: *ta stoicheia tou kosmou.*
14. Greek: *ta asthenē kai ptōcha stoicheia.*

could not be measured or explained by lining up its teachings with Him, for they did not match. The heretical teachers had substituted "human tradition" and "elementary practices" in place of Christ. As a result, any who were ensnared would be led away from Christ.

3. The Content of True Doctrine (2:9-15)

a. Christ possesses fullness of deity. (2:9)

VERSE 9. Why should the Colossians need a new philosophy or additional ceremonies? Christ alone possesses everything essential. "In Him all the fulness of deity dwells in bodily form" (NASB). The expression "all the fulness" was used previously in 1:19 (see discussion). Now it is further clarified as a reference to the very essence of deity. The word *theotēs* used here denotes the Godhead in its essence, as distinguished from a similar word *theiotēs*, which denotes the divine attributes or characteristics.[15]

This fullness of deity has a present and permanent dwelling in Christ. The verb (*katoikei*) denotes a permanent residence rather than a temporary sojourn, and its present tense indicates that this situation continues to be so.

The adverb "bodily" (*sōmatikōs*) has been understood in a variety of ways. Some have interpreted it to mean that deity is "embodied" in Christ, not diffused among angels; according to this interpretation, the word has no special reference to the incarnation.[16] Others have explained the term as if it meant "really" or "actually," and find a parallel in the contrast between "shadow" and "body" (*sōma*) in 2:17,[17] although there is no other evidence for such a use of the adverb. The best explanation treats the term in its most obvious sense as referring to Christ's incarnation but also including His present glorified

---

15. The term *theiotēs* occurs in the New Testament only in Rom. 1:20, where it indicates that the heathen may know God by His attributes in creation around them. But only in Christ is the personal essence of God (*theotēs*) revealed.

16. E. K. Simpson and F. F. Bruce, *Commentary on the Epistles to the Ephesians and the Colossians* (Grand Rapids, 1957), p. 232, footnote; William Hendriksen, *Exposition of Colossians and Philemon* (Grand Rapids, 1964), p. 112.

17. Arndt, p. 807.

Fig. 7. Laodicea (north theater), with Hierapolis in distance. *Levant*

body.[18] By comparison with 1:19, it is clear that the "fullness" resided in Christ as the eternal image of God before and apart from the incarnation. In 2:9 Paul adds the thought that this fullness was also resident in Christ when He assumed a human body. The present tense of the verb is appropriate, for Christ continues to possess all the fullness of deity in His present glorified body.

    b. Believers have received all they need in Christ. (2:10-15)
      1) Believers have been made full in Christ. (2:10)
    VERSE 10. The meaning of "made full" (*peplērōmenoi*) must be influenced by the sense of "fullness" (*plērōma*) in the preceding verse. Christ possesses all the fullness of God, and believers are "in Him." Hence they partake of His fullness, and have no lack which ritual, angelic mediators, or other factors must supply. The same thought is expressed elsewhere:

> And of his fulness have all we received, and grace for grace. (John 1:16)

---

18. This is the view of Lightfoot, Abbott, Lenski, Carson, and Johnson.

And to know the love of Christ, which passeth knowledge, that ye might be filled with all the fulness of God. (Eph. 3:19)

Till we all come in the unity of the faith, and of the knowledge of the Son of God, unto a perfect man, unto the measure of the stature of the fulness of Christ. (Eph. 4:13)

The verb "made full" or "made complete" is a perfect passive tense form which indicates that the work has been done and the resultant condition continues. Believers are in vital union with the very One who has already supplied them with all they could ever need to qualify them for God's approval. Paul reinforced the point by reminding his readers that it is Christ who is the head over all spirit beings. In 1:16 Paul showed that Christ had created all such beings. In 2:10 he repeated two terms from the list which represent the whole group. How foolish to assign any saving function to angelic mediators! Christ is head over them all, and inasmuch as believers are in Christ and draw upon His fullness, they have no need to look to angels to supply any deficiencies.

2) Believers were spiritually circumcised in Christ. (2:11-12)

VERSE 11. The false teachers at Colosse may have emphasized the importance of Jewish circumcision. They did stress other Jewish rites (2:16), and earlier false teachers in Galatia had urged physical circumcision (Gal. 5:1-12). Paul's reply to the Colossians was that they had already been circumcised, even though most of the Christians there were Gentiles. It had not been, however, a physical operation, for it had occurred "without hands." He referred to spiritual circumcision, which he called elsewhere a circumcision of the heart (Rom. 2:29). Even the Old Testament repeatedly stated this concept of an inward spiritual circumcision (Deut. 10:16; 30:6; Jer. 4:4; 6:10; 9:26; Ezek. 44:7, 9). The apostle defined it not as merely a removal of a portion of flesh, but removal of "the body of the flesh." Since it has already been indicated that physical flesh and its removal cannot be meant here, the reference must be to "flesh" as a metaphor for the sinful self (compare the similar use of "flesh" in Gal. 5:19-21), and the "body of the flesh" means the entire "old man" (3:9). This removal occurs at conversion when the miracle of new birth strips away the old nature as the dominating force in the life, and the "new man" is created (3:10).

This is further explained as occurring "in the circumcision of Christ." It refers to the spiritual circumcision which Christ performs (*tou Christou* is here regarded as a subjective genitive), and is another name for regeneration. This seems clear from the fact that 2:13 indicates "uncircumcision" to be the state of spiritual death; "spiritual circumcision" must therefore refer to the impartation of spiritual life. It is Christ's act that is in view, not that physical rite imposed by the Mosaic legislation.[19]

VERSE 12. Paul explained how this spiritual circumcision, that is, regeneration, came about. It occurred by virtue of believers' identification with Christ in His burial and resurrection (see also 3:1-3). The reference to "baptism" is commonly explained as indicating water baptism, which pictures the identification of the believer with Christ in His death, burial, and resurrection. It would be strange, however, for Paul to make such a point of a circumcision made without hands (that is, an act that was not physical) and then urge its replacement with simply another physical action. It is better to regard the reference as indicating Spirit baptism, in light of the spiritual circumcision just discussed. Paul referred to that act of God whereby believers are baptized with the Spirit into the body of Christ (I Cor. 12:13). A helpful parallel is Romans 6:3-4:

> Know ye not, that so many of us as were baptized into Jesus Christ were baptized into his death? Therefore we are buried with him by baptism into death: that like as Christ was raised up from the dead by the glory of the father, even so we also should walk in newness of life.

This must refer to Spirit baptism, for not all who go through the water rite are actually placed into the body of Christ. Only those who put their faith in the operation of God who raised Christ from the dead are identified with God's Son, and are made

---

19. Another view explains "the circumcision of Christ" as referring to the death of Christ, in which He put off "the body of His flesh" (1:22), and with which death believers are identified (3:3). F. F. Bruce, *Colossians*, p. 234. However, the explanation given in this exposition seems more likely.

participants in the redeeming effects of His death and the regenerating life of His resurrection.

3) Believers have been forgiven in Christ (2:13-15)

VERSE 13. Regeneration involves a gracious forgiveness of transgressions. Before their conversion, these people had been spiritually "dead," and this condition had manifested itself both in the deeds they were committing which violated God's standards ("transgressions") and in their possession of a fleshly nature which was hostile to God ("the uncircumcision of your flesh"). They were sinners by nature and by practice.

It was to such people that God had granted new life ("made you alive," NASB) by identifying them with Christ ("with Him"). Man's sinfulness had separated him from God and brought about this state of spiritual deadness. By identifying believers with Christ who paid sin's penalty by His death, God has forgiven all transgressions. The word "forgiven" (*charisamenos*) is part of the word-family which also includes the term "grace" (*charis*). It reminds us that this is a gracious forgiveness on God's part, not due in any sense to the merits of the sinner.

VERSE 14. This forgiveness involved the canceling of man's debt to God. "Handwriting" (KJV) or "certificate of debt" (NASB) translates a word commonly used for an acknowledgment of a monetary obligation.[20] It was so called because the debtor usually signed it (see Fig. 14). In this instance the bill of indebtedness had to do with the "decrees" or ordinances of God. The same term is used in Ephesians 2:15, where it clearly refers to the Mosaic law. In Romans 2:14-15 it is clear, however, that the law of God is written in the hearts of Gentiles as well. In the present passage both Gentiles and Jews are in view, and hence the reference is to God's broken law, whether as codified by Moses or given generally to all men.

This bond of indebtedness to God was "against us" (*kath' hē-mōn*). Man was on the debit side of the ledger. Furthermore, it had become "hostile to us" (*ho ēn hupenantion hēmin*). This is

---

20. Adolph Deissmann, *Light from the Ancient East* (Grand Rapids, reprinted 1978), p. 332.

a stronger expression than the preceding one and it could be illustrated by an unpaid bill turned over to a bill collector. So God's broken law hounds the sinner at every turn, pursuing him through an accusing conscience as well as by Scriptural warnings.

But God, however, has done something about the problem. First, He has erased the debt. Christ's death was sufficient to completely cancel the bond against the sinner. Second, He has removed the bill itself from its position as a barrier between Himself and sinners. The perfect tense "has taken" (*ērken*) implies not only the historic act of Christ's sacrifice but its permanent effects. It is still so! Third, the bill of debt was nailed to the cross and it perished along with Christ. A more forcible way of depicting man's release from sin's debt can hardly be imagined.

VERSE 15. The forgiveness of believers also involved the removal of angelic powers. Two views are commonly encountered on this passage. One explanation regards the "rulers and authorities" (KJV, "principalities and powers") as evil angels who were disarmed by the victory of Christ at the cross.[21] The cross was the public demonstration (for those who would heed it) of God's vanquishing of satanic forces (John 12:31; 14:30). The "triumphing over them" suggests the homecoming parade of a victorious Roman general who was granted the honor of a parade called a "triumph," with the bound captives and spoils of battle forming part of the procession.

This view, however, is not without its weaknesses. The same words "rulers and authorities" were used just a few verses earlier in 2:10, where they clearly referred to good angels, not evil ones. Also the middle voice of the participle *apekdusamenos* does not mean "having disarmed someone" but "having divested himself of something." Hence it does not properly describe the taking of power away from evil angels. Furthermore, the only other New Testament occurrence of the verb "to triumph" (*thriambeuō*) does not imply a triumphing "over" the direct object but a leading in triumph "with" (II Cor. 2:14).

---

21. This view is well expressed by Lightfoot, *Colossians*, pp. 190-92.

What may be a better interpretation, therefore, regards good angels in view in 2:15, just as in 2:10.[22] At the cross God divested Himself of the angelic mediators through whom He had given the law (Acts 7:53; Gal. 3:19; Heb. 2:2), and this particular function was now retired. This accords well with 2:14, as well as with the larger context (see on 2:8) and with Pauline thought generally (Gal. 3:24-25), where the law is regarded as now superseded. These angelic mediators of the law are thus regarded as part of Christ's "triumph," since they had fulfilled their function. Even the translation "triumphing over them" is no real problem to the "good angels" view, since in the metaphor just used Paul has depicted the God-given law which was against us as nailed to the cross.

The closing phrase of the verse should probably be rendered "in Him," referring to Christ as the one in whom all of this was accomplished.[23] This phrase, which occurs repeatedly in verses 6 through 15 emphasizes the centrality of Christ to the Christian faith. To Him and Him alone do we look for the salvation that means approval with God.

Questions for Discussion

1. How does one "walk" in Christ?
2. In the light of Colossians 2:8, is it wrong to study philosophy?
3. What are some ways that religious charlatans deceive the unwary?
4. In what sense are believers made full or complete in Christ?
5. What does Paul mean by a circumcision made without hands?

---

22. This is the view of A. S. Peake, "The Epistle to the Colossians," *The Expositor's Greek Testament*, ed. W. Robertson Nicoll (Grand Rapids, reprinted), III, 528-530; Wendell E. Kent, "The Spoiling of Principalities and Powers," *Grace Journal*, Vol. 3, No. 1 (Winter, 1962), pp. 8-18.

23. The words *en autōi* could be translated "in it," referring to the cross. This is usually suggested by those who understand that the subject of the sentence has shifted from God the Father (v. 13) to Christ. The view taken in this exposition, however, regards God as the subject throughout the passage.

7

Three Deadly Errors

COLOSSIANS 2:16-23

The Colossian heresy has thus far been described as a deceptive philosophy that was human, not supernatural, in origin (2:8). It was characterized by elementary religious practices that were limited to the temporal world scene. How foolish it would be for anyone to let himself be captivated simply by persuasive talkers, and forget the true spiritual treasures which are found in Christ (2:3, 9-15).

In 2:16-23 Paul became more specific as he described the doctrinal errors that were being promoted by some in Colosse and its neighboring cities. The religious philosophy at Colosse placed special emphasis upon certain rituals and observances, and upon the need to worship angels. Furthermore, it fostered an ascetic spirit among its followers, whereby harsh treatment of the physical body was regarded as sanctifying. The apostle saw these as deadly errors, utterly valueless to save or to produce strong Christians; the Colossian heresy actually threatened to defraud believers because it would rob them of the real spiritual progress which God had planned for them.

As present-day Christians consider this passage, it should remind them that these same deadly errors are still very much alive. They appear in different guises at various times, but religious practitioners have always been skillful at making these practices seem attractive, reasonable, and "spiritual." Paul's rebuttal to the Colossians still stands as a much-needed warning to which every Christian should give careful attention.

C. The False Doctrines of Men (2:16-23)

1. The Warning against Ritualism (2:16-17)

a. The command (2:16a)

VERSE 16a. "Therefore" (*oun*) indicates that this command is based upon the previous discussion. There it had been shown that the law which condemned us has been erased, removed from its place, and nailed to Christ's cross. The angelic mediators of the law were now no longer involved in that function.

Consequently, the command was, "Let no one act as your judge" in the various matters of ritual about to be named. The particular form of the command[1] may imply that the practice was presently going on and must be stopped. The only basis for anyone to pass a judgment upon Christian behavior regarding these matters was the assumption that the Mosaic law still held its condemning force against them. Since this was no longer true (2:13-14), believers must not let themselves be fooled into thinking that someone's judgment against them in these matters has any biblical warrant.

b. Some examples (2:16b)

VERSE 16b. Five items of ritualistic observance were chosen by Paul to pinpoint the sort of erroneous criticism which the Colossian Christians were not to tolerate. First, they were not to put up with any adverse judgment concerning eating (*en brōsei*). The noun refers to the act of eating, not just the food which was eaten, but the Jewish differentiation between clean and unclean foods does seem to be involved.[2] Believers were being told that they were still obligated to observe the Jewish dietary regulations, and that anything less was contrary to Scripture and thus liable for judgment.

---

1. Greek: *mē krinetō*. The present imperative with *mē* can denote an order to cease an action that is in progress.

2. To treat "eating and drinking" solely as a reference to asceticism is to introduce a somewhat awkward mingling of this nonbiblical practice with the other Old Testament items of verse 16. It is better, therefore, to regard asceticism as discussed in verses 20-23, and to see "eating and drinking" in verse 16 as a general reference to the insistence upon Levitical distinctions in their dietary habits.

Christ, however, taught that foods themselves were neither moral nor immoral (Mark 7:18-19). Even a Jew in Old Testament times who violated the law and ate pork was not spiritually contaminated by the pork itself, but by his disobedience to God. Pork was not sinful; disobedience was. Thus when the law's demands were satisfied at Calvary, such ritualistic distinctions had no more force. This truth was not understood immediately by Jewish Christians. It took a direct revelation in a vision before Peter realized that "what God hath cleansed, that call not thou common" (Acts 10:15).

Second, believers were not to put up with efforts to impose Judaistic requirements upon them regarding drinking. The law of Moses had less to say about drinking than eating. Nevertheless, it did lay down certain requirements for priests ministering in the temple (Lev. 10:9), the storage of liquids in unclean vessels (Lev. 11:34, 36), and for those taking Nazirite vows (Num. 6:3).

The third example was "a matter of a festival." The term *heortē* was the regular one for the great annual religious feasts of the Jews, such as Passover, Pentecost, and Tabernacles.

Paul's fourth mention was the "new moon," the monthly Jewish celebration which was held in connection with their lunar calendar. Frequent mention is made of it in the Old Testament and special regulations were given for its observance (e.g., Num. 10:10; 28:11; I Sam. 20:6, 18; Ps. 81:3; Hos. 2:11; Amos 8:5).

The fifth matter of ritual observance which some were advocating was the Jewish sabbath day.[3] This was the weekly festival held from sundown on Friday evening until sundown on Saturday. Some groups today still advocate this observance, while calling themselves Christian. But even the practice of calling Sunday the "Christian sabbath" has no warrant in Scripture, and could become an example of the very thing Paul

---

3. The Greek form *sabbatōn* is plural. However, it was apparently a transliteration of the Aramaic, rendered in Greek as *sabbata* (with the final *aleph* being rendered as an *alpha*). When the word was inflected, therefore, plural forms were used. That the term was actually regarded as a singular is clear from Josephus, *Antiquities* 3.10.1. See J. B. Lightfoot, *St. Paul's Epistles to the Colossians and to Philemon* (Grand Rapids, reprinted), p. 194; T. K. Abbott, *The Epistles to the Ephesians and to the Colossians* (Edinburgh, 1974), p. 264.

denounced at Colosse if its observance is made an obligatory practice with duties demanded and judgments pronounced.

c. The explanation (2:17)

VERSE 17. Christians were not to let themselves be coerced into practicing these things because such rituals were just a shadow of what was coming. The terms *skia* and *sōma* are obviously used to contrast the "shadow" and the solid "body" which casts it. The Old Testament ceremonies were a foreshadowing of certain realities which were yet to occur, but they had no validity apart from the "body" or substance which they foreshadowed.

The "body," said Paul, belongs to Christ.[4] Christ is the One to whom the Old Testament types and shadows pointed. Now that Christ has come, the shadows are no longer needed. The apostle was not speaking of Christ's physical body, nor His spiritual body which is the church, but of the reality as opposed to the shadow. The same truth was expressed earlier in Galatians 3:24-25, where Paul explained that the Mosaic law acted as a tutor until Christ, but since Christ has come the tutor is no longer involved. The law had fulfilled its function. It was Christ who with His plan of salvation cast the shadow in Old Testament times to prepare men for His coming. All the types and shadows are fulfilled in Him. How foolish, then, to hang on to the shadows when the reality has come!

Christians sometimes have difficulty in distinguishing between the clear commands of the New Testament, and the "legalism" which is frequently denounced. We must recognize that when Christians are told that they are free from "the law" (Gal. 5:1), that does not mean that they are under no obligation to God (Gal. 5:13). The "law of Christ" rests upon every Christian, and he is expected to fulfill what his Master commands (e.g., Gal. 6:2). "Legalism" is best understood as a spirit which fails to recognize that God's grace has made us acceptable to Him, and that human works have no part in it. God's grace has made believers into new creatures whose delight is to do out of love what pleases their Father. It is a false notion that a list of policies (most of which are only indirectly related to Scriptural

---

4. Greek: *to de sōma tou Christou.*

commands) can be rigidly imposed upon believers to make them more acceptable to God (or to their scrutinizing brethren). Compliance so often leads to false pride; noncompliance creates a censorious spirit among the critics.

2. *The Warning against Angel Worship* (2:18-19)

a. The command (2:18a)

VERSE 18a. The imperative verb *katabrabeuetō* occurs only here in the New Testament. Other members of the same word-family are *brabeus*, *brabeutēs*, meaning "umpire," and *brabeion*, "prize." Whether the verb specifically contains the idea of denying the prize to someone, or is used more generally with the sense of "deciding against" is uncertain because of the rarity of the word. At the very least, the command of Paul was, "Let no one rule against you" (parallel in thought to the command in 2:16), and it may be that the more specific idea was involved, "Let no one keep defrauding you of your prize" (NASB). The believers at Colosse were not to allow anyone to divert them with false teaching, and thus cause them to waste precious time that should have been spent in spiritual progress—progress that would ultimately bring its reward from Christ.

b. The promoter of angel worship (2:18b-19)

VERSE 18b. Four characteristics describe such a false teacher, and Paul set forth each with a participial phrase in the original text. First, a false teacher acts merely by his own will to emphasize "humility" and worship of the angels. The Greek text is very difficult here, and has led to various interpretations. Ignoring the extreme view that all manuscripts of this passage are wrong and hence a new conjecture must be offered, one still has two reasonable possibilities. The phrase *thelōn en* may be taken to mean "delighting in,"[5] describing the individual as taking pleasure in his "humility." The explanation which may be better, however, treats *thelōn* as a modal participle, "acting by his mere will."[6] This is similar to its use in II Peter 3:5 ("will-

---

5. This is a Septuagintal phrase, found in such passages as I Sam. 18:22. Although an increasingly popular interpretation, it is strongly opposed by Abbott, *Colossians*, p. 267, as being totally without parallel in Paul's writings.

6. This is suggested also by the ASV margin.

fully"), and also agrees well with the thought in the Colossians context where these people were accused of "self-made religion" (2:23).

This man-originated philosophy promoted the idea of worshiping angels, presumably as a display of self-abasement. Probably it was suggested that God was too holy and remote to be directly approached by sinners, and therefore angels should be worshiped as intermediaries. In the process Christ must have been displaced as the sole mediator between God and man (I Tim. 2:5).

Second, such a teacher was taking a stand on things which had been seen. Again the Greek text is very difficult because several rare words have been employed. However, there has been growing agreement since the studies of Sir William Ramsay that the participle *embateuōn*, from its background in Phrygia, should be understood as a religious term referring to one who had entered upon a higher level of experience.[7] This person could then promote his knowledge by "taking his stand on what he has seen,"[8] either as a claim to have seen visions, or else as a reference to the physical and material "elementary" things of the world involving religious ceremonies which he found so attractive (2:8).

Third, he is "vainly puffed up by the mind of his flesh." He has an inflated opinion of himself, but it is without adequate cause. He has not estimated his spiritual knowledge on the basis of biblical and apostolic teaching, but upon the promptings of his fleshly mind. Because his intellect is controlled by "his flesh," that is, his old nature, rather than by the Holy Spirit, his notions are faulty, and his confidence is unjustified.

VERSE 19. Finally, he is not holding fast to the Head. It is Christ, the Head of the spiritual body (the church, 1:18), who is the life-giving source for all the body's needs. Just as the head of a physical body supplies support so that the various parts can function normally, so Christ is the support of His church for all that she needs. As the head gives unity to the body and controls

7. W. M. Ramsay, *The Teaching of Paul in Terms of the Present Day* (London, 1913), pp. 283-305.

8. This translation is based upon the omission of the negative which appears in KJV. Most of the preferred manuscripts omit *mē*.

its movements through the junctures and ligaments which enable the various limbs to move in coordination, so Christ as the Head of the church makes it a spiritual unity with each member fulfilling a helpful function toward every other member. And as the head controls the growth of the physical body through the pituitary gland attached to the brain, so Christ controls the spiritual growth of the church in order that it may grow with the "growth which is from God" (NASB).

Anyone who does what these at Colosse were doing is not in connection with the Head. Hence he is not getting his direction from the Head, and cannot be experiencing the spiritual growth which only the Head can produce. He is like the one Jesus described, "If a man abide not in me, he is cast forth as a branch, and is withered; and men gather them, and cast them into the fire, and they are burned" (John 15:6).

3. The Warning against Asceticism (2:20-23)

a. The errors of asceticism (2:20)

VERSE 20. Asceticism is that religious philosophy which teaches that depriving the physical body of its normal desires is a means of achieving greater holiness and approval from God. Such practices as fasting, celibacy, withdrawal from society, abandonment of possessions, and even self-flagellation are employed in varying degrees.

It must be recognized that the Bible gives a place to proper self-discipline. Fasting was practiced occasionally, even by Jesus (Matt. 4:1-2). Certain values in celibacy were recognized by Paul (I Cor. 7:32-35). The problem comes when these practices are viewed as intrinsically more holy than their counterparts, when they are forced (either formally or informally) upon others, or when they become an end in themselves. These very things were happening at Colosse, and Paul dealt with them by pointing out three of the errors of that ascetic teaching.

First, it ignored the fact that believers had died with Christ. The phrase "if you have died with Christ"[9] does not cast any doubt upon the Colossians' experience; Paul was, in fact, making it the basis for his argument. The readers had put their trust

9. A first class condition, using *ei* with the indicative.

in Christ as the Savior who had died in their place. Consequently, God had counted them as having died when Christ died
(2:12; 3:3; Rom. 6:1-10).

This identification with Christ in His death had separated them
"from the elementary principles of the world." As noted in the
exposition of 2:8 where the same expression was used, this
referred to various ceremonial practices which were being
insisted upon at Colosse. Some of the practices were derived
from the Old Testament law and were being imposed on Christians. Certain false teachers apparently ignored the fact that
Christ's death had totally satisfied God's broken law, and
believers' union with Christ in His death meant that they were
now dead to those obligations.

Second, this ascetic teaching was forcing believers to continue
living in the realm of this world system to which they had died.
The words, "why as if you were living in the world," shows the

Fig. 8. Colosse, side of mound. *Levant*

unreasonableness of this procedure. It is true that the Colossian believers still *were* in the world, but their *living* now was energized by the new spiritual realm to which they belonged. They had risen with Christ (2:12), so as to walk in newness of life (Rom. 6:4). To place believers under the ceremonies that were part of the past was to make them to be "living in the world" rather than in the energy of their regenerated life in Christ.

Third, asceticism was placing decrees upon believers. The verb *dogmatizesthe* can be rendered with the interrogative pronoun as: "why are you letting yourselves be subjected to decrees?"[10] The fact that a past tense was not used may indicate that the process was not complete. The pressure was on but they had not thus far yielded (note 2:5). The verb is part of the same word-family which includes *dogma*, the term used in 2:14 to mean the divine ordinances against sinners which were canceled at the cross. In 2:20 it also includes the demands of the ascetic teachers which are illustrated next.

b. Some examples of asceticism (2:21)

VERSE 21. Three examples of the decrees being urged by these religious philosophers are given in a climactic order, with the first term being the strongest. A paraphrase would be: "Don't handle this! Don't taste that! Don't even touch this other thing!" In his selection the apostle has picked regulations having particular reference to foods. However, it should not be concluded that the ascetic emphasis was limited to such matters. We really do not know what the total list of taboos contained at Colosse.

c. The inadequacy of asceticism (2:22-23)

VERSE 22. Asceticism is not the way to become holier, and Paul shows its inadequacy in principle by three observations. First, these very prohibited items perish through normal usage. "Which all are to perish with the using." The particular reference here is to food items which loom so large in any ascetic system. Everything which an ascetic philosophy would

---

10. This translation treats the verb as a permissive middle.

forbid being touched or eaten was headed for eventual decay by being used up. Jesus had taught this as well:

> Do you not see that whatever goes into the man from outside cannot defile him; because it does not go into his heart, but into his stomach and is eliminated? (Thus He declared all foods clean.)
> Mark 7:18-19 (NASB)

How can such things have authority over man if he can destroy them by using them up?

Second, the apostle noted that such decrees were of human origin. "In accordance with the commandments and teachings of men" should be taken with verse 20. These decrees were not part of God's Word but were human inventions (2:8). The language here seems indebted to our Lord's discourse recorded in Mark 7:1-23 (note v. 7), which in turn was drawn from Isaiah 29:13.

VERSE 23. Third, Paul asserted that these practices have no value for curbing the appetites of the flesh. To be sure, they have a certain reputation[11] of wisdom in ascetic circles. When one is operating in the realm of "self-made religion" (*ethelothrēskiāi*; compare 2:18, "acting by his mere will") and emphasizes self-abasement, any show of self-discipline especially to the point of severe treatment of the body is usually impressive to onlookers. The Oriental mystic, the "holy man," the religious monk, and the resident of the convent all present an appearance of great dedication and piety. However, Paul said that this was "not with any value toward satisfying the flesh."[12] These ascetic practices—avoiding wholesome foods, mistreating the body—do not exterminate the appetites of the flesh. The old nature of flesh is opposed to God and will seek to gratify itself. Mere harshness

---

11. This expression uses *logos* in the sense of appearance, estimation, or report (Arndt, p. 478).

12. The original text at this point is sufficiently difficult that Peake, as well as others, has resorted to the despairing conclusion that we are dealing with a primitive corruption and that no emendation thus far is convincing ("The Epistle to the Colossians," *The Expositor's Greek Testament*, III, 536). The view given in this exposition is based upon the following considerations: (1) *pros* normally means "with a view to," or "toward." There is little warrant here for the meaning "against." (2) *plēsmonēn* means "satisfaction" or "gratification." It does not necessarily connote excessive indulgence. Hence the sense can be that ascetic habits do not satisfy the flesh so that it ceases its sinful cravings.

to the physical body will not solve the problem because the seat of the sinful nature lies in the heart of man (Mark 7:20-23). The ascetic who supposes he can deny himself material comforts, withdraw from sinful society, and thereby achieve a state of holiness is deceiving himself. He merely finds that he has taken his sinful heart with him, and the old flesh is still unsatisfied.

The answer to the quest for a more holy life is not to be found in such an approach, but in a recognition of what Christ has provided. Only when the believer understands that Christ has furnished everything he needs (2:9-13) and then trusts Him for the energy to live effectively (2:6-7), can he make spiritual progress with the growth which is from God (2:19).

Questions for Discussion

1. What is the difference between legalism and obedience to the commands of Scripture?
2. What is the difference between asceticism and a proper avoidance of sensuality?
3. What is wrong with asceticism?
4. How many contemporary examples can you cite of legalism? angel worship? asceticism?

8

The Principle for Christian Living

COLOSSIANS 3:1-4

Many Christians have a problem with the Christian life. After the passing of time, their faith seems to lose its attractiveness. Initial enthusiasm dwindles away. The excitement over their new commitment no longer seems as stimulating. As a result some become disillusioned. They have regarded Christianity simply as a creed—a statement of beliefs to be acknowledged—but nothing more than that. Their lives soon settle down into their previous routines, and those looking on would never suspect they were Christians.

Frequently, however, they are not content to live with their present needs unsatisfied. Having found mere creedal statements devoid of any real dynamic for living, they begin to search for something else. Wherever such a search develops, someone or some movement inevitably arises to meet it. Every cult that has plagued the Christian church developed because there were Christians who failed to understand what true Christian faith really means. Nearly every new "formula for Christian living" or "secret of success" is an effort to capitalize on the dissatisfaction of Christians who have somehow failed to understand what the Bible teaches about the Christian life.

Scripture is clear that there is a practical side to Christian doctrine. Christianity is not just a creed. It is a "Way" (this was one of the earliest names that Christians used for their movement[1]). Conversion implies a changed life. Consequently, the

---

1. See Acts 9:2; 19:9, 23; 22:4; 24:14, 22.

believer must never forget that his salvation experience involves much more than just a past event in his life. That was merely the beginning. The new birth initiates the believer into a life to be lived. It provides the dynamic to energize this new life, and continual guidance from the Scripture to direct it along the proper channels. Only when the Christian ignores what God has provided does he find his Christian faith a disappointment.

The early Colossians faced the same challenge. They would either respond in faith and obedience to the teaching of Christ and the apostles, or they would soon feel a lack and be enticed to follow man-made schemes that would ultimately lead them far astray. It was to the problem of Christian living that Paul addressed the section that follows in this epistle.

III. EXHORTATIONS TO PRACTICAL CHRISTIAN LIVING (3:1—4:6)

A. The Basic Principle for Christian Living (3:1-4)

1. Believers Were Raised with Christ (3:1)

a. The condition (3:1a)

VERSE 1a. "Therefore" (*oun*) points to the material just preceding in which the apostle set forth the errors that confronted his readers. Neither legalistic ritual, nor angel worship, nor ascetic regimens could provide the sort of life which pleases God. In fact the believers had "died" to such things (2:20). Consequently they were now in a far different condition.

The author's assumption was stated as a conditional clause, "If then you have been raised up with Christ." In form it is what Greek grammarians commonly call a first class condition.[2] Paul was not casting any doubt upon their relation to Christ, but was using this assumption as the basis for his exhortation.

The verb "raised" is not a reference to the believer's future resurrection from the dead, but to his identification with Christ's resurrection following the crucifixion. It describes a past occurrence. This same thought has already been expressed by Paul in this epistle when he described believers as "buried" with Christ

---

2. The first class condition uses *ei* (if) in the protasis with the verb in the indicative mood.

and "raised up" with Him (2:12), and as "made alive together with Him" (2:13). The reference can be properly understood only by beginning with the historical event of Christ's death and resurrection (2:12). It was that occasion when Jesus Christ acted as the sinner's substitute which provided the foundation for Paul's explanation. God in His grace chose to identify every believer with His Son. This identification, however, is experienced by the believer when he puts his faith in Christ and is converted (2:12).

Thus Paul was not referring to a future resurrection event, nor to a mystical religious experience that is the possession of a few. He was describing rather a condition that is true of every genuine believer. Every person who has been born again has been "raised up with Christ." It is Christ's resurrection which secured both immortality (Rom. 6:9) and a newness of life (Rom. 6:4). Therefore when a person trusts Christ to save him, not only are Christ's righteous merits applied to him but he also becomes a sharer in that newness of life which Christ's resurrection obtained. This was the situation which Paul understood existed in Colosse.

b. The command (3:1b)

VERSE 1b. On the basis of Christians' sharing of Christ's resurrection life Paul exhorted them to "keep seeking the things above." The form of the verb emphasizes the continuing obligation. Because believers have been raised with Christ, they must continually guide their activities and energies in a new direction. "Seek" (*zēteite*) implies here not an investigation but an effort to obtain. Every Christian is to be concentrating his efforts upon developing these characteristics which have their source in the spiritual life from above. No longer must he be lured by the attractions of the "elementary principles of the world." Certainly he must not follow the desires of the flesh. The person raised with Christ must be living the life of Christ.

As a further reminder of the direction our lives should take, Paul described "the things above" as located "where Christ is." Inseparably tied to the resurrection of Christ was His ascension to heaven. It is implied, therefore, that in our identification with Christ in His resurrection we continue to be identified with Him now, which places believers with Christ above. In the companion Epistle to the Ephesians Paul wrote that God has "raised us up with Him in the heavenly places in Christ Jesus" (2:6). Believers are residents and citizens of a new realm. The fullest experience of this fact must await Christ's return and the believer's physical resurrection and glorification, but even now every believer is in spiritual union with Christ; that fact is basic to his daily Christian living. Our lives must take a new direction in view of our relationship to Christ.

The additional thought is expressed that Christ is not only "above," but is also "seated at the right hand of God."[3] This is the position of majesty and authority. This truth was first expressed in the Messianic reference in Psalm 110:1, "The Lord said unto my Lord, Sit thou at my right hand, until I make thine enemies thy footstool." The psalmist David quoted Jehovah as addressing the Messiah ("my Lord") in these words which Jesus later indicated had reference to Himself (Matt. 22:41-46; Mark 12:35-37; Luke 20:41-44). To this position Jesus has already been exalted by virtue of His resurrection and ascension. Believers have been made sharers of His resurrection life and are in such a vital union with Him that it can be said they are seated with Him in heavenly places (Eph. 2:6). This should provide the dynamic as well as the incentive for developing in their lives those things which pertain to the spiritual realm above.

2. Believers Died with Christ (3:2-3)

a. The command (3:2)

VERSE 2. "Set your mind on the things above" (NASB) stresses the importance of one's mindset. The previous imperative, "keep seeking" (*zēteite*) referred to the concentration of one's energies and activities. This command (*phroneite*) requires that the thoughts and attention also be continually directed toward this goal of the things above. A person's actions are the result of his thinking. The mind directs activities by the decisions it makes. That is why Paul regards it as extremely important that the Christian have the proper mental attitude, and

---

3. Because of word order, it is better to regard the participle *kathēmenos* not as part of a paraphrastic verb, but as expressing an additional thought.

Fig. 9. Hierapolis main street, view north (archaeologists' tram tracks). *Levant*

that the objects upon which his thinking is focused be worthy (see Phil. 4:8).

"The things above" are not limited to the future life in heaven, for the succeeding verses (especially vv. 12-17) clearly pertain to activities to be pursued on earth. The apostle is referring to those thoughts which find their source and their direction in the new life which believers share with Christ above. These are the concepts which are wholesome and edifying because the regenerated life which Christ bestows has provided new goals, new insights, and a new mindset whose object is holiness.

This sort of goal is in contrast to "the things upon the earth." The reference is to those matters of purely earthly and temporal concern. Some unworthy objects of the Christian's interest are clearly sinful. Various evil practices, such as those named in verses 5-9, should always be avoided. There are other earthly things, however, which are not in themselves sinful, but which can be dangerous and detrimental if they capture the attention of the Christian and divert him from pursuing spiritual goals of far greater value. This is especially true in the case of ascetic practices and other forms of legalism. It is not sinful to fast, or to deny oneself physical comforts, or even to study the philosophies of men. But when these things lure the Christian's attention from the truth which God has revealed, or cause him to develop habits of thought which emphasize these earthly matters and hinder the development of a mindset which centers on spiritual concerns ("the things above"), such things are harmful to the Christian's growth.

b. The explanation (3:3a)

VERSE 3a. Although the translation "for ye are dead" (KJV) is well known, it is not the most accurate rendering of this statement. The verb form here does not name the present state but a past occurrence.[4] A better translation is "for you died." In this context there can be little doubt that the reference is to the believer's identification with Christ in His death at Calvary (2:20; 3:1). This event not only secured for believers the full satisfaction of God's righteousness and the forgiveness of sins, but also served to sever the connection which had bound them as sinners to elementary religious teachings which characterize the world scene (2:20). That former life had left them under condemnation, and their only prospect was death. It was by the incomparable wisdom and plan of God that He chose to send His Son as the sinbearer in man's stead. When Christ died, God counted believers as being in His Son. When He died, they died, and the benefits become theirs by faith when they are born again. Hence the old life which once was responsive only to the allurements of sin is gone. It died with Christ. It is for this reason that believers' minds should be centered on new goals, and their conduct should reflect this new way of thinking.

c. The consequences (3:3b)

VERSE 3b. At first reading, the words "and your life" appear to be a contradiction, for the apostle has just written that his readers had "died." The context, however, has declared that

---

4. The form is the aorist indicative, *apethanete*.

the believer has not only died with Christ, but has risen with Him. As a consequence he possesses a resurrection life with the Savior.

This new life "is hid with Christ in God." To describe the believer's life in this manner is to indicate that it is doubly safe. It is hidden away with Christ, and He is seated on the right hand of God (v. 1) in heaven. Surely there could be no safer refuge than this. To have one's life hid with Christ in God is to be in vital association with the One who is in heaven as a forerunner, guaranteeing the safe arrival in due time of all who are in Him (Heb. 6:20).

To have one's life hidden with Christ also implies that it is unobserved by others. This explains why those outside of Christ fail to understand the true situation of the child of God. They often think him to be odd or fanatical. They may recognize differences between his conduct and their own, but there is no understanding of the regeneration that has occurred. This is due, said Paul, to the fact that the believer's new life is presently hidden. Some of its effects can be seen, but they are often misinterpreted. It will not, however, be this way always, as the writer points out next.

3. Believers Will Be Displayed with Christ (3:4)

a. The time of this display.

VERSE 4a. The spiritual realities which are presently true for believers must be accepted by faith. Many of them involve truths which cannot be seen except with the eye of faith. The believer's position in Christ, his regenerated life, the forgiveness of his sins, and his death to the old life that was under condemnation—none of these can be examined with the natural eye and demonstrated with scientific proofs. Paul has explained the reason: the believer's new life is presently hid with Christ.

A time is coming, however, when all will be made public and clear. That time will occur when Christ returns. The verb "shall appear" (phanerothēi) is apparently used synonymously by Paul with the word "reveal" (apokaluptō).[5] The root idea is to make

---

5. Rudolph Bultmann and Dieter Luhrman, "Phaneroō," TDNT, IX, 4-5. Attention is called to Ephesians 3:5 and Colossians 1:26 where apokaluptō and phaneroō are used respectively in these parallel passages.

visible what is invisible. The reference here is to Christ's return, at which time He will be revealed visibly to the world. His present glory is hidden from earthly view, but that future day when He returns will end the present obscurity.

"When" is actually "whenever" (*hotan*), introducing an indefinite relative clause of time. It suggests no doubt about the fact of Christ's return, but only uncertainty regarding the time. Paul set no dates. He did not know exactly when Christ would return in glory, but whenever it would occur, at that time ("then") believers would also experience a visible display of their true spiritual condition.

This Christ who will be displayed at His coming is described as "our life" (*hē zōē hēmōn*).[6] In this statement He is not merely depicted as the bestower of life, but as the life itself. Paul has mentioned this earlier in the epistle (1:27), as well as in his other writings (Gal. 2:20; Phil. 1:21). The apostle John quoted Jesus as saying the same thing: "I am the way, the truth, and the life" (John 14:6). Hence more is involved than merely identification with Christ. In actuality our life *is Christ*, who lives within each believer and is the very essence of the eternal life which Christians even now possess. When this fact is recognized, one has all he needs as the basis for Christian living. The believer must accept this by faith at present, but this can provide him with all the power with which to live effectively, as well as supplying him with the incentive to perform the kind of daily living which will reflect the new person he is.

b. The persons who will be displayed (3:4b)

VERSE 4b. Not only will Christ be made visible when He returns in glory in the culminating phase of His second coming, but Paul reminded his readers, "You also will be revealed with Him." No longer will they be despised and misunderstood. No

---

6. An alternative reading which has equally good manuscript support uses *humōn* (your) rather than *hēmōn* (our). Both KJV and NASB have adopted *hēmōn*, probably on the grounds that *humōn* was a scribal change to make the statement conform to the expression "your life" in verse 3, and the subject "you" of the verb in the following clause. It must also be noted that it is not uncharacteristic of Paul to shift from the second person to the first person when he is discussing a theme in which he has personal involvement along with his readers (see 1:10-13; 2:13; Eph. 2:13-14; 5:2; I Thess. 5:5).

longer will their faith be disregarded as mere wishful thinking. Faith will become sight, and the realities in which believers have trusted but cannot see will become visible not only to them but to all the world. Paul reverted to the second person "you," probably because he was trying to inspire them by this prospect. They did not need to yield to any enticements from Judaizing and ascetic teachers in order to win favor with God. Through their identification with Christ and their sharing of His life, they already possessed the basis for proper Christian living. In due time at Christ's return this would be made clear and visible to all. Meanwhile they should recognize their position in Christ and live in the light of its implications.

c. The nature of this display (3:4c)

VERSE 4c. Christ's return will reveal Him and His followers "in glory." The veil which obscures that glory from shining forth today will be removed. Christ's bodily absence which now keeps men from seeing the glory which He resumed at the ascension (John 17:5; Acts 1:9) will be a barrier no more. As for believers, the gradual transformation into a greater Christ-likeness which is occurring today from one stage of glory to another (II Cor. 3:18) will be completed when they see Him. The essence of this glory in which Christians will be displayed is the glory of Christ Himself which they will reflect without the sinful defilements which now mar that reflection. The apostle John wrote similarly, "Beloved, now are we the sons of God, and it doth not yet appear what we shall be: but we know that when he shall appear, we shall be like him; for we shall see him as he is" (I John 3:2).

The basic principle for Christian living, then, has been supplied for us. No need exists to search for something new. In Christ, God has provided all that is needed for approval with Him and for godly living on earth. All that remains is for the Christian to recognize what God has done and act upon its implications. Christ Himself is now our life. When this is realized, the believer's thoughts and actions will reflect a different attitude. Conduct will be altered. Christian faith will become not just a creed but a life that trusts God and proceeds according to His will.

Questions for Discussion

1. How does one become "raised up with Christ"?
2. What are "the things above" which Christians should seek?
3. In what sense did believers die with Christ?
4. What are the implications of having one's life hidden with Christ?
5. What changes will occur when believers are revealed with Christ in glory?

9

The Procedure for Christian Living

COLOSSIANS 3:5-17

Christianity is more than a creed. It is a life. It is not confined to hymns and prayers and creedal recitations, but involves the continual response of the believer to the new life which regeneration has created in him.

The joy of Christian living, however, is not shared or understood by all. To some, being a Christian is explained solely in terms of religious ceremonies. Going to church, taking communion, and participating in special observances at Christmas and Easter are all that their Christianity implies to them. Very little difference appears in their daily lives.

Others are looking for some dramatic spiritual "experience" which is supposedly at the center of all Christian living. They search for a "baptism," and explain Christian living only in such terms. These also fail to grasp the biblical instruction that is really very clear. Paul's explanation should leave no doubts about how Christians are to live, and how they should accomplish a biblical lifestyle. Already in Colossians he has laid down the principle that undergirds all Christian living (3:1-4), the fact that every true believer has died with Christ and has risen with Him. Paul has pointed out (as an incentive) that Christians will someday share the glory of Christ at His return. Next he set forth what the believer's responsibility is. Paul called for no mystical experience, no dramatic "baptism," no secret enlightenment available only to a few. The procedure is obvious and simple. The problem is that so many are lax in doing it.

113

B. The Proper Method of Christian Living (3:5-17)

1. *Put Off the Vices of the Old Man* (3:5-11)

a. The command (3:5a)

VERSE 5a. "Put to death your members which are upon the earth" is a literal rendering of Paul's phrase. The imperative (*nekrōsate*) does not have the connotations that the word "mortify" now does (KJV), nor is it limited to a merely mental process, "consider as dead" (NASB). It denotes rather the putting forth of effort, and means to kill, put to death. Here it is used with reference to the believer's bodily parts (*ta melē*), which are viewed metaphorically as the sins which are committed through our bodies. Every Christian is to put to death the sins which so easily monopolize the activity of our bodies. Inasmuch as Paul has already laid down the principle that believers have died with Christ (3:3), the passage must be understood as teaching that the Christian's practice must be brought into conformity with his position. Our minds should be centered on things in heaven (3:2); hence we must sever ourselves from the sinful activities of earth. We did die with Christ. Now we must display this fact in daily living.

b. The old vices (3:5b)

VERSE 5b. Five sins are named to illustrate Paul's meaning.[1] "Immorality" (*porneian*) is a word that denotes illicit sexual conduct, including fornication and adultery. "Uncleanness" (*akatharsian*) forms a pair with the preceding term, but is more general. It denotes impurity in any form. Sometimes it may convey the idea of perversion (Rom. 1:24), but it regularly implies a condition that alienates the sinner from God.[2]

"Passion" (*pathos*) in this context denotes erotic passion, as in all its New Testament uses (see Rom. 1:26; I Thess. 4:5).[3] It is closely allied with "evil desire" (*epithumian kakēn*). "Desire" itself can be good or evil, depending upon the

---

1. It is simplest to regard these accusatives as appositional with *melē* (members). We understand them to be instances of metonymy, in which effect is substituted for cause. Another possibility treats them as accusatives of specification: "Put to death your members . . . in regard to fornication," etc.

2. Friedrich Hauck, "Akatharsia," TDNT, III, 427-29.

3. Wilhelm Michaelis, "Pathos," TDNT, V, 926-30.

legitimacy of the object desired. Here it is plainly "evil desire," and although this can express itself in almost limitless ways, the emphasis in the context is on sexual desire.

The last vice mentioned is "the greed which is idolatry" (*tēn pleonexian hētis estin eidōlolatria*). Greed (literally, wishing to "have more") can refer to all sorts of materialistic desires. However, there is strong reason to understand the greed here as having sexual overtones. The previous items in this list refer to sexual sin. Furthermore, the comparable verb form is used by Paul of coveting ("defraud," KJV) a brother's wife (I Thess. 4:6). This should not surprise us when we recall that the Old Testament commandment against covetousness in the Decalogue was stated in these terms: "Thou shalt not covet thy neighbor's wife" (Exod. 20:17). Greed is idolatry because such overpowering desire to possess what is not rightly one's own relegates God to a secondary place.

c. The reminder (3:6-7)

VERSE 6. Sin should always be shunned because it violates the command of God. Furthermore, Paul reminded his readers that God's holy and unchanging wrath always stands poised against it, and merely awaits the proper time to be unleashed.[4] The sinful world is already condemned, and God's wrath upon it is inevitable (John 3:36). Inasmuch as the believer is no longer under condemnation, but has passed from death to life, sinfulness should no longer be his practice.

VERSE 7. Paul reminded his readers that these sinful practices had characterized their former lives as unbelievers: "In them[5] you also once walked" (NASB). "Walking" describes behavior, and although it need not be concluded that every convert had previously committed every sinful act just mentioned, it is true that unbelievers are all pursuing their activities in this sort of atmosphere. They had "walked" that way because they "were

---

4. The words "upon the sons of disobedience" are omitted here by certain major manuscripts, such as P46 and B, and perhaps are an interpolation from Eph. 5:6, where they properly belong. The tendency today among Greek editors and in recent English versions is to omit the phrase.

5. The pronoun "them" (*hois*) is regarded as neuter, referring to the list of sins in verse 5, rather than as masculine referring to "sons of disobedience" (see footnote 4).

living" in that realm. Because they had been spiritually dead (unresponsive and helpless toward God), their conduct had naturally reflected the worldly existence to which they were limited.

d. Some additional vices (3:8-9a)

VERSE 8. In contrast to what they "once" (v. 7) had been doing, "now" they should "put off" all such sinful practices. The change that had come about in their lives since their conversion to Christ should have been sufficiently distinct and so immeasurably better that no longings for the old life should remain.

"All these" (KJV) things which must be discarded included the list in verse 5, as well as the additional list in verses 8-9. This second listing centers upon sins which involve the wrong use of speech. First to be mentioned are wrath (*orgēn*) and anger (*thumon*), those attitudes of the heart which usually lie behind the sins we commit with our tongues. "Wrath" denotes the settled attitude. It need not be sinful, for God Himself can display wrath in an absolutely holy manner (3:6). Man's wrath, however, is rarely untinged with less worthy motives. The Epistle of James warned Christians to be "slow to wrath; for the wrath of man worketh not the righteousness of God" (James 1:19b-20). Too frequently man's wrath involves personal animosity and revenge.

The term "anger" denotes the tumultuous outburst of passion. The two words are interrelated; each one can lead to the other. An attitude of wrathfulness can erupt in an angry outburst, or a brief display of anger can settle into a permanent state of hostility. With man, most displays of anger cannot be kept within the bounds of holiness. So-called "righteous indignation" is far rarer than its claimants would admit.

"Malice" (*kakian*) is a general term for badness, and can denote ill-will, an evil deed, trouble, or wickedness. It was used of the materialistic request of Simon Magus (Acts 8:22). Here it refers to the evil actions that result from misdirected wrath and anger.

"Blasphemy" (*blasphēmian*) in some contexts describes a speaking that defies God. However, the term in the Greek world was not so restricted, and could denote injurious or abusive speech, whether against God or man. Here it seems unlikely that any direct blasphemy of God was in the writer's view inasmuch as he was writing to Christians. More likely he was directing his words to the harmful speech which Christians can all too easily hurl at one another.

"Shameful speaking" (*aischrologian*) was likewise to be put out of their mouths. The reference is to a speaking which is dishonorable, disgraceful, filthy, or abusive. It must have been just as easy for the early Christians as it is for us to let their tongues express ideas, suggestions, or judgments that should have no place in a holy life.

VERSE 9a. Although this final admonition against the misuse of speech might have been added as a sixth term in the list just enumerated, it is given as a separate statement. "Lie not to one another." How frequently Christians let this characteristic of the "old man" appear in their lives. The present imperative prohibits the practice of lying.[6] The idea is, "Never be lying to one another." Distorting the truth, deceiving others through one's speaking, and outright lying are totally inconsistent with Christian profession, which involves identification with Christ who is "the way, the truth, and the life" (John 14:6).

e. The explanation (3:9b-11)

VERSE 9b. The reason why such practices could no longer be indulged is that these believers had already put off "the old man with his deeds." The "old man" refers to all that is inherited from Adam, apart from the regenerating touch of God. It is the sinful, fleshly nature which is possessed by every person through physical birth. In this passage, Paul does not tell his readers to "put off"[7] the old man, but makes the fact of their already "having put off the old man" (*apekdusamenoi ton palaion anthrōpon*) the basis of his appeal. At the time of their regeneration this had been done. They had dethroned the "old man" as the dominating principle in their lives. Consequently their Chris-

---

6. The present imperative with *mē* sometimes implies stopping an action already in process (i.e., "Stop lying"). This is by no means invariable, however, and it is doubtful that Paul would intimate that the Colossian Christians were continually lying to each other.

7. Although it is sometimes urged that the aorist participle here should be treated as an imperative and thus be similar to the thought expressed in Eph. 4:22 (e.g., Lightfoot, *Colossians*, pp. 214-15), it is more likely that the participle should be regarded as causal, giving the reason for the exhortation.

tian practice was to be brought into conformity with their new position in Christ. The coupling of the words "with his deeds" to the act of renunciation of the "old man" makes it clear that the salvation experience even at its outset implies a changed lifestyle. The unregenerate nature was characterized by various evil practices, and these were renounced in principle when the Colossians became Christians.

VERSE 10. At the same time that the old man was put off, the "new man" had been put on. "New" (*neos*) means young, that which did not exist before. The old nature cannot be reformed; it must be replaced. The "new man" is the regenerated self which has been united with Christ so that Christ dwells in the believer. This too was not something which was being urged upon the readers, but was an accomplished fact which was to motivate their conduct.

The new man is described as "being continually renewed unto a full knowledge." This is the process of present sanctification whereby the believer grows in his knowledge of God and His will (1:9) and becomes more Christ-like in his thoughts, words, and deeds. Paul expressed the same thought elsewhere in these words: "But though our outer man is decaying, yet our inner man is being renewed day by day" (II Cor. 4:16). It is a gradual growth as the believer continues to look with faith at his Lord: "But we all, with unveiled face beholding as in a mirror the glory of the Lord, are being transformed into the same image from glory to glory, just as from the Lord, the Spirit" (II Cor. 3:18).

"After the image of him that created him" recalls the language of Genesis 1:26-28. God created man in His image, but man's fall into sin has grievously marred that image. It takes the regenerating work of God through Christ to bring about a restoration. Christ Himself is the perfect image of God (1:15), and by virtue of being united with Him believers have the prospect of having their lost position ultimately restored (Heb. 2:6-10). Meanwhile the transforming work is presently going on as the "new man" (which each believer now is) experiences continual renewal after God's own image.

VERSE 11. In the new man mere earthly distinctions are irrelevant. The categories "Greek and Jew" divide people on the

Fig. 10. Ruins at Hierapolis. *Levant*

basis of nationality or race. Yet it is not one's race which makes him acceptable to God, nor does that make of him a new man (see Acts 10:34-35). One should read Ephesians 2:11-22 for a fuller discussion of the removal of distinctions between Jew and Gentile.

The next pair of terms, "circumcision and uncircumcision," contrasts religions. Circumcision was the pride and distinction of Judaism, and the Colossian Judaizers doubtless boasted of their acceptance of this rite (*contra* 2:11). Paul had written an earlier epistle in which he had carefully and forcibly pointed out the error and danger of insisting upon circumcision as a spiritual advantage (Gal. 5:2-12).

The terms "barbarian, Scythian" reflect a Greek point of view, being the way a Greek or Roman might describe the rest of the world. They are examples of cultural distinctions. Even these are irrelevant in making men acceptable to God. A "barbarian'' (*barbaros*) was one whose language was foreign, and among the Greeks it denoted anyone ignorant of the Greek language and culture. A Scythian (*Skuthēs*) was regarded as the lowest type of barbarian. These people were nomadic invaders from the Black Sea and Caspian Sea areas. The historian Herodotus in the fifth century B.C. described them as follows:

> During the twenty-eight years of Scythian supremacy in Asia, violence and neglect of law led to absolute chaos. Apart from tribute arbitrarily imposed and forcibly exacted, they behaved like mere robbers, riding up and down the country and seizing people's property.[8]

> . . . The Scythians, however, though in most respects I do not admire them, have managed one thing, and that the most important in human affairs, better than anyone else on the face of the earth: I mean their own preservation. For such is their manner of life that no one who invades their country can escape destruction, and if they wish to avoid engaging with an enemy, that enemy cannot by any possibility come to grips with them. A people without fortified towns, living, as the Scythians do, in waggons which they take with them wherever they go, accustomed, one and all to fight on horseback with bows and arrows, and dependent for their food not upon agriculture but upon their cattle: how can such a people fail to defeat the attempt of an invader not only to subdue them, but even to make contact with them?[9]

As regards war, the Scythian custom is for every man to drink the blood of the first man he kills. The heads of all enemies killed in battle are taken to the king; if he brings a head, a soldier is admitted to his share of the loot; no head, no loot. He strips the skin off the head by making a circular cut round the ears and shaking out the skull; he then scrapes the flesh off the skin with the rib of an ox, and when it is clean works it in his fingers until it is supple, and fit to be used as a sort of handkerchief. He hangs these handkerchiefs on the bridle of his horse, and is very proud of them.[10]

. . . They have a special way of dealing with the actual skulls—not with all of them, but only those of their worst enemies: they saw off the part below the eyebrows, and after cleaning out what remains stretch a piece of rawhide round it on the outside. If a man is poor, he is content with that, but a rich man goes further and

8. Herodotus, *The Histories*. Translated by Aubrey de Selincourt (Middlesex: Penguin Books, 1972), pp. 84-85.
9. Ibid., p. 286.
10. Ibid., p. 291.

gilds the inside of the skull as well. In either case the skull is then used to drink from.[11]

The final pair, "slave, free man," refers to social opposites. This distinction permeated the society of the ancient world. However, it is without significance to the new man. In Christ all are brothers. That is not to say that such social distinctions did not impose particular responsibilities upon the earthly lives of Christians (see 3:22-4:1). But they had no essential, eternal significance. In the spiritual realm from which the new man draws his life, no such distinctions exist.

For the new man, Christ is "all and in all." "All" (*panta*, literally "all things") refers to all that the new man needs for birth and growth. Christ is the One who supplies every requirement. No dependence need be placed on such things as race, religious tradition, culture, or social class. Furthermore, Christ is "in all" (*en pasin*). If this term is regarded as neuter ("in all things") as in the previous use, Christ is understood as permeating all the relations of life. It could, however, be masculine ("in all persons"), and refer to the fact that Christ is the One who indwells every believer, regardless of earthly status. The parallel in Galatians 3:28 argues for the latter.[12]

2. Put On the Virtues of the New Man (3:12-17)

a. The command (3:12a)

VERSE 12a. By addressing the readers as "elect of God, holy and beloved," Paul was reminding them of their incomparable position. They had been selected by God, set apart from a sinful world, and made the objects of His matchless love. Remembering who they were would encourage them to live how they ought to live.

b. The new virtues (3:12b-17)

VERSE 12b. Because believers have put on the new man (3:10), they must put on the characteristics of the new man. It is not enough merely to put off various vices (3:8). These must be

---

11. Ibid.
12. S. Lewis Johnson, "Christian Apparel," *Bibliotheca Sacra*, Vol. 121, No. 481 (January, 1964), p. 28.

replaced by positive virtues if their Christian faith is to be properly displayed.

The list is begun with the naming of five qualities without additional explanation. "A heart[13] of mercy" (*splangchnon oiktirmou*) describes one's sensitivity to those suffering or in need. "Kindness" (*chrēstotēta*) is sweetness of disposition, the attitude which should characterize the believer's dealings with others. "Humility" (*tapeinophrosunēn*) is the view of oneself which every Christian should display. "Meekness" (*praütēta*) is the opposite of harshness or arrogance. "Longsuffering" (*makrothumian*) is the opposite of revenge. All of these Christian attitudes are concerned with the welfare of others and a willingness to subordinate oneself.

VERSE 13. Believers are also responsible to endure and forgive the actions of others. "Forbearing" (*anechomenoi*) means to put up with, endure, or bear with. It conveys the idea of holding oneself erect under the burdens imposed by others. The Christian, however, must go beyond resignation and also be "forgiving" (*charizomenoi*).

The implication is that Christians sometimes have conflicts among themselves ("one another"). The church is not perfect. Nevertheless the believer who has a complaint against another Christian, whether justified or imagined, is obligated to endure it and to forgive graciously. The passage does not indicate that confession must first be secured from the offender. Public forgiveness may await public repentance, but causes of complaint are to be responded to with a forgiving spirit.

This principle of enduring and forgiving was clearly taught by Jesus (Matt. 18:21-22). It was also practiced by Him. The great example of this attitude was Christ's forgiveness of sinners on the basis of His sacrifice at Calvary. "Even as Christ forgave you, so also do ye." The believer's attitude must be evaluated by no less a standard than Christ Himself.

VERSE 14. The believer is responsible to put on love. Although no verb is expressed, the grammatical form of the

---

13. The Greek term *splangchnon* denoted literally the visceral organs, which were the part of the body to which the seat of emotions were ascribed. The comparable English metaphor is "heart."

word "love" (*tēn agapēn*) indicates that it is an object, and the most obvious verb to supply is "put on" (from verse 12).

"Above all these things" (KJV) or "beyond all these things" (NASB) may indicate the supreme importance of this Christian virtue. However, the phrase (*epi pasin de toutois*) can mean "on top of all these things," and may be a continuation of the figure of getting dressed (i.e., "put on"). If so, the love commanded here is being viewed as the final article of clothing which completes one's spiritual attire.

This love is said to be the "bond of completeness" (*sundesmos tēs teleiotētos*).[14] It is like the belt which keeps all the rest of one's apparel in place. The thought is similar to what Paul expressed in I Corinthians 13:1-3, where all other virtues are properly exercised only if love is present. This love always has the benefit of others in view, and only when it is displayed can the believer be said to have the completeness or maturity which God desires of him. It is produced by the Holy Spirit within the believer (Gal. 5:22), and Christ Himself is the Christian's supreme example (John 13:34).

VERSE 15. Christians must let the "peace of Christ" be their umpire. In times of disagreement among believers, each one should let his desire for the peaceful atmosphere which Christ provides determine his decision. A. S. Peake expressed it in these words: ". . . in deciding on any course of action, let that be chosen which does not ruffle the peace within you."[15] The verb "rule" (*brabeuetō*) means to act as arbiter or umpire. This implies that there may be occasions when Christians will disagree. The proper course is for each believer to desire the continuation of Christ's peace in his own heart, and this will avoid strife or disunity in the larger assembly. Unilateral action is unthinkable, for believers have been formed into "one body" (see also Eph. 4:2-4). Christ's peace should, therefore, characterize the whole as well as the individual member.

---

14. The lack of a clear antecedent that is grammatically acceptable for the neuter pronoun in the phrase *ho estin* is explained either as (1) an instance of "sense" agreement in which "love" is viewed as a "thing" rather than as a feminine noun, or else (2) it is equivalent to "that is." Similar uses in the latter sense appear in Mark 14:42 and 15:42. A. T. Robertson, *Word Pictures in the New Testament* (New York, 1931), IV, 504.

15. A. S. Peake, "The Epistle to the Colossians," EGT, III, 541.

This desire for peace should not, however, be a reluctant acquiescence for purposes of harmony. Believers should wholeheartedly pursue it and "be thankful." Recognition of the divine operation within them ("the peace of Christ") and realization of the creation of the "one body," of which Christ Himself is the head (1:18) should prompt the positive response of thankfulness. It is when God's grace has been forgotten that the joy of thanksgiving disappears from the Christian's life.

VERSE 16. Believers must let Christ's[16] Word dwell in them richly. This is the only New Testament occurrence of the phrase "the Word of Christ," although references to "the Word of the Lord" and "the Word of God" are frequent. It appears to be equivalent to "the teaching of Christ," and would include not only His earthly words recorded in the Gospels, but all of Scripture, to which He gave His authority.

For the Colossians to let Christ's Word dwell richly in them was to let it be at home in their hearts individually, and to let His teachings have full impact in every plan and every decision. In order for this to occur, the Word of Christ had to first be taken into the heart. Christ's teaching cannot be a factor in our plans unless we know what He teaches. Here then is a scriptural injunction for every Christian to familiarize himself with all the Word of God.

The church is also responsible to engage continually in teaching, admonishing, and singing. Three participles convey this thought, which is expressed in two parallel phrases. The phrase, "with all wisdom teaching and admonishing yourselves with psalms, hymns, spiritual songs" (literal), has been punctuated in various ways (the oldest manuscripts have no punctuation at all). It seems best to relate "with all wisdom" with what follows, inasmuch as Paul uses the same phrase with the identical participles in 1:28.[17]

"Teaching" is the positive aspect of instruction, the imparting of truth. "Admonishing" is the negative aspect in which warnings are given concerning the standards and obligations of

16. Although some manuscripts read "God" or "Lord" at this point, the preponderance of early evidence argues for "Christ" as the true reading.

17. Furthermore, this preserves the parallelism with the following participial phrase which is introduced with *en chariti* (with thanks).

God's word. Both must be performed "with all wisdom" if they are to be effective. If it seems strange to urge Christians to teach others by the songs they sing, one should compare Ephesians 5:19 where the same point is made: "Speaking to one another in psalms and hymns and spiritual songs, singing and making melody with your heart to the Lord." The word "psalms" (*psalmois*) denotes songs sung with musical accompaniment. Here the reference may be to the inspired psalms of the Hebrew Old Testament. "Hymns" (*humnois*) are songs which address praise and glory to God. "Spiritual songs" (*ōidais pneumatikais*) is a more general reference to songs of a spiritual nature. In the early church the use of song could serve, just as it does today, as a most effective tool to convey the truth of God's revelation in an attractive and easily remembered way.

This singing should be done "with thankfulness[18] in your hearts" (NASB). Such expressions of praise must not be from the lips only, but should be the overflow of hearts which have recognized God's truth and desire to praise Him for it.

VERSE 17. In summation, the believer is exhorted to do everything in the name of the Lord Jesus. The imperative verb "do" is not actually expressed, but is clearly implied from the subjunctive clause "whatever ye do."[19] This performance includes everything in the realm of thought and action. Nothing is outside its scope. The Christian's mental activity and his actual performance of deeds should be "in the name of the Lord Jesus." Our realization of who the Lord Jesus is, our identification with Him, His authority over us, and a recognition of His will for us should govern all Christian thought and activity. At the same time, continual thanksgiving should be rendered to God who has transformed our lives through the saving work of Jesus Christ and has given ability and opportunity to live in a manner pleasing to Him.

Paul has thus answered the need of the Colossians for instruction in daily living, not by imposing a list of ceremonies or legal

---

18. The translation "with thankfulness" is simpler in this passage than "with grace" (KJV), and is a legitimate use of *chariti*. See I Cor. 10:30.

19. The introductory phrase *kai pan ho ti ean poiēte* (and whatever ye do) is an independent nominative (sometimes called nominative absolute), as in Matt. 10:32, Luke 12:10, and John 17:2.

taboos as the heretical teachers in Colosse were doing, but by pointing them to Christ. He gave no new code of rules with penalties attached, but reminded them what God had done for them in Christ. Now as a "new man" in Christ, each believer needed only to ask what conduct was appropriate for the one who was identified with Christ. The principles of this sort of conduct are clearly taught in Scripture. It is the believer's responsibility to apply them to every thought and deed of life.

Questions for Discussion

1. If Christians have already died with Christ, why must they still put to death various practices?
2. What is the "old man"?
3. What is the "new man"?
4. What are the responsibilities of the Christian in times of disagreements with other Christians?
5. What standard should govern the Christian's thoughts and activities?

10

The Christian Household

COLOSSIANS 3:18—4:6

After setting forth the principles (3:1-4) and procedures (3:5-17) of Christian living, Paul applied them to the basic unit of society, the family. To him the Christian faith was not simply a religious exercise to be performed on stated occasions; it was a life-transforming experience which affected every aspect of the believer's existence.

This approach to Christian living was fundamental in apostolic teaching. The New Testament contains numerous passages where instruction was given to Christian households, directing each member to perform his role in the light of his Christian commitment.[1] Obviously the Christian faith was not merely a new religion to be added to an otherwise unaffected pagan lifestyle, but was a way of life that had implications for every human relationship.

In Colossians 3:18—4:6 Paul exhorted six specific classes of people, grouped into three pairs. Underlying his discussion was the principle of authority, and in each pair he first addressed the subordinate member (wives, children, slaves) and then the one in authority. It should also be borne in mind that *Christian* households are in view, not those of unbelievers.

---

1. See also Eph. 5:22—6:9; I Tim. 2:8-15; 6:1-2; Titus 2:1-10; I Peter 2:18—3:7.

C. Some Specific Relationships in Christian Living
(3:18—4:1)

1. Wives (3:18)

VERSE 18. One should read the parallel in Ephesians 5:22-24
to gain additional understanding of this passage. The term
gunaikes was used for "women" generally, or for "wives." The
context makes it certain that the meaning "wives" is intended in
this passage. They are exhorted to be subject[2] to their husbands. The apostle was not saying that all women should be
subject to all men, but that wives should be subject to their husbands (see Eph. 5:22). No intimation is given that this subjection
is based upon inferiority in intelligence, morality, spirituality,
worth, integrity, or any other quality. It is a relationship referring solely to authority.

The explanation given is that such action "is fitting in the
Lord." The subordination of the wife to the husband is not a
popular viewpoint today (perhaps it never has been and that was
why Paul discussed it). Nevertheless it is frequently taught in
Scripture (Eph. 5:22-24; I Peter 3:1-6; Titus 2:5). The tense of
the verb "fitting" implies that this was no recent or temporary
circumstance, but has always been God's arrangement for the
human family.[3] It is an obligation which comes from the past.
Even before the Fall, creation itself taught us that God's intent
was for the woman's role to be supportive of her husband (Gen.
2:18; I Tim. 2:12-13). God's pronouncement after the Fall reinforced the original plan which Eve had violated (Gen. 3:16b).
Women who are "in the Lord," that is, who are Christians and
thus are guided by the Lord's instruction, will be characterized
by this sort of conduct.

2. Husbands (3:19)

VERSE 19. A more extended Pauline treatment of this subject

---

2. It makes little practical difference whether the verb *hupotassesthe* be
regarded as a passive ("be subject") or as middle ("subject yourselves"). The
result is the same in either instance, and the wife is the one responsible for making herself subject to her husband's authority.

3. A. T. Robertson calls the imperfect *anēken* (was fitting) "an idiomatic use
of the imperfect indicative with verbs of propriety in present time." *Word Pictures in the New Testament* (New York, 1931), IV, 506.

occurs in Ephesians 5:25-33. In Colossians Paul limited himself to two admonitions. First, husbands must love their wives. Although wives were commanded to be subject to their husbands, the husbands were not to treat them as subjects but to love them. This love (*agapate*) goes beyond natural affection and seeks always what is best for the wife. It is the sort of love which will sacrifice for one's beloved (John 15:13) and will always be unselfish (I Cor. 13). The great example for Christian husbands is Christ Himself, the bridegroom who loved the church without reserve (Eph. 5:25).

Husbands are also enjoined not to develop a bitter attitude toward their wives. The verb is used of water which has been made bitter (Rev. 8:11). It is also used of an incensed and angry attitude, when one is mastered by a bitter spirit.[4] Perhaps Paul had in mind instances where a husband might develop a continuing resentment because of a wife's lack of submissiveness. Each partner must not only do his part in a positive way to strengthen the marriage tie, but must also refrain from wrong responses which will only aggravate unfortunate situations.

3. *Children* (3:20)

VERSE 20. Again Paul first exhorted the subordinate party in the couplet. (For a similar treatment, see Ephesians 6:1-3). Addressing the children, he urged them to *obey* their parents. The original sense of this verb was "to hearken at the door,"[5] and it was employed of one who responded to a knock on the door and came to listen (Acts 12:13). It came to mean hearkening to a command, obedience.

This responsibility of children to obey is to both parents (*goneusin*). All of the direction and discipline in the home should not be left to one parent. Both are responsible under God to give guidance to the children, and the children are obligated to obey mother as well as father.

The obedience called for here applies to "all things." No exception is indicated. Must a Christian child do wrong if a sinful parent commands it? It may be properly assumed that Paul un-

---

4. Wilhelm Michaelis, "Pikros, *et al.*," TDNT, VI, 125.
5. Gerhard Kittel, "Hupakouō," TDNT, I, 223.

derstood Christian parents to be involved from the way he next addressed the fathers. This should avoid most such problems. However, the Scripture teaching is clear that human authority is never absolute, and that in cases of conflict, God must be obeyed rather than man.[6] Paul was not here discussing every conceivable situation, but was laying down a principle. Exceptional cases must be worked out individually in the light of that principle.

Obedience to parents is "well pleasing in the Lord." It pleases God because it accepts the biblical standard which has been given to mankind (Exod. 20:12).

4. *Fathers* (3:21)

VERSE 21. A similar injunction occurs in Ephesians 6:4. The term "fathers" (*pateres*) was sometimes used of both parents (as in Heb. 11:23), and this would be appropriate here since the children were instructed to obey both parents (3:20). However, the change from the term *goneusin* (parents) to *pateres* (fathers) in this paragraph may have been deliberate. Fathers, as heads of the households, have the final responsibility for directing the children's behavior, and thus were specifically addressed.

A literal translation of the command could be: "Do not be continually irritating your children." Paul was not so naive as to suppose that fathers (and mothers too) can avoid all instances of conflict with their growing offspring. Total permissiveness is not a biblically-based philosophy. There will be times of unpleasantness, and children will become annoyed and irritated when disciplined. What Paul was prohibiting was the habitual provoking of children by insensitive parents. Continuous faultfinding with no respite should not characterize the Christian home.

The danger is that ceaseless irritating of the children may create a sullen, listless, discouraged disposition. A child who experiences continual criticism and rarely any love will be scarred for life. Christian practice in the home will display the balance which creates a wholesome climate and well-adjusted children.

---

6. Peter wrote that one is obligated to obey every government order (I Peter 2:13-15). Nevertheless he also taught that if obeying the government would require a believer to disobey a clear command of God, then he must obey God and accept the consequences (Acts 4:19; 5:29).

5. *Slaves* (3:22-25)

VERSE 22. The parallel account is in Ephesians 6:5-8. More space is devoted by Paul to the discussion of the responsibilities of slaves and masters than to any of the other groups in this list. Furthermore, the discussion in this epistle and its companion Ephesians is more extended than in Paul's other letters (*contra* I Tim. 6:1-2; Titus 2:9-10). The reason for this emphasis in Colossians (and Ephesians) was the presence of Onesimus who would accompany the epistle. The church, and especially other slaves in the membership, would have a keen interest in the apostle's instruction regarding this delicate matter.

Slaves in the church were first commanded to give continuing obedience to their human masters. This applied to "all things." The command is the same as that given to the children (3:20). The Christian slave was not at liberty to choose when and where he would be obedient (with the single exception of an order to commit sin, Acts 5:29). Conversion to Christ, even though it made every believing slave and master equally a "new man" (3:10-11), did not obliterate all earthly distinctions (for example, it did not eradicate the present difference between male and female, Gal. 3:28). In spite of the injustice of slavery, Paul did not urge revolution. Rather he taught principles of right and wrong which eventually caused the slave system to die wherever Christianity went.

A grudging or half-hearted compliance with the master's wishes would not suffice. The phrase "not with eyeservice as menpleasers" refers to work that is performed only as long as the master's eye is upon the worker. At such times the slave might try to appear very diligent to please his owner, but that would fall far short of the integrity which the Christian ethic requires. Performance was to be with "singleness of heart, fearing the Lord." "Singleness" (*haplotēti*) refers to that which is simple, unambiguous, pure, or sincere.[7] It is the opposite of double-dealing and hypocrisy. The Christian slaves were not only to respect and obey their earthly lords, but were to recognize their continuing need to reverence the heavenly Lord.

---

7. Otto Bauernfeind, "Haplous, Haplotēs," TDNT, I, 386-87.

They were not to be concerned merely with pleasing men, but were to fear God in all their service.

VERSE 23. The second exhortation to Christian slaves urged them to regard their work as a sacred duty. This applied to "whatever you do," no matter how mundane and insignificant it might appear. They were to do their work "heartily" (literally: "out of the soul"). They were to put their hearts and souls into it. The expression reaches beyond a perfunctory performance and calls for honest, whole-hearted effort. Whenever daily labor is viewed "as for the Lord and not to men," a new dimension is brought into view. Yet this is not mere make-believe, for the Christian is ultimately responsible to God for how he uses the time and energy which has been given to him. As long as work is honorable (and the Christian should engage in no other kind), honest toil should be viewed as a dignified and even sacred duty, whether in the slave-master system of an earlier day, or in the employee-employer relationship today.

VERSE 24. An explanation was given to the slaves to encourage their compliance with these instructions. Actually it was a reminder of something they already knew: "Knowing that from the Lord you will receive the reward of the inheritance." This may imply that these teachings were part of a core of the apostles' teaching (Acts 2:42) with which most churches were familiar. These slaves needed to keep in mind that they would be rewarded by their heavenly Lord. Earthly slave owners might not be fair, but the service of the Christian slave had implications that went far beyond the current social system.

"The reward of the inheritance" is best understood as "the reward consisting of the inheritance"[8] (compare 1:12). In earthly terms, slaves did not inherit. A kindly master might leave a bequest to a fortunate slave, but the slave was not an heir in the usual sense of the term. A Christian slave, however, was an heir of God, and was qualified to receive an inheritance which included every blessing that awaits believers.

Paul added the phrase, "the Lord Christ you are serving."[9]

---

8. "Inheritance" (*klēronomias*) is regarded as an appositional genitive.

9. The verb can be either indicative (as treated in the exposition above) or imperative: "Keep serving the Lord Christ." Either way, the slave is reminded that his real service is to the Lord and not to men.

Earthly demands might obscure this truth, so Paul reminded the slaves of this spiritual reality. Rewards might not be forthcoming from earthly masters. Injustice might be all too frequent, for unappreciated work was more the rule than the exception. But the eyes of the slave were to look upward, and receive encouragement from the faith that their menial service for an earthly master could be viewed in a far different and more exalted light.

VERSE 25. Paul further explained that God will ultimately adjudicate all wrongs, and He will do so without respect of persons. "For he who does wrong will receive the consequences of the wrong which he has done" (NASB). Does this refer to the unjust slave owner, whose ultimate punishment by God is assured, and therefore the mistreated slave should leave the matter with Him?[10] Or was it a reminder to the slave that he should serve honestly since God will ultimately deal with offenders?[11] Actually, it is best to regard it as a statement of a principle which is universally true, and applies equally to slave and master.[12] This understanding is reinforced by the similar statement in the companion epistle: "Knowing that whatever good thing each one does, this he will receive back from the Lord, whether slave or free" (Eph. 6:8).

"And there is no respect of persons," said Paul. In a human setting the slave might have expected the master to be preferred because of power and prestige. Or he might have thought that when God judges, He will excuse the slave simply because he is a slave. Paul's point was that God is absolutely impartial. God judges on the basis of what is right, not on outward appearance or superficial considerations.

Although slavery as an institution no longer exists in the Western world, the principles taught in this passage have obvious application to the employer-employee relationship today.

6. *Masters* (4:1)
VERSE 1. Similar instruction occurs in Ephesians 6:9. The

---

10. The view of Abbott, *Colossians*, pp. 295-96, and Carson, *Colossians*, pp. 94-95.

11. The view of Peake, "Colossians," p. 543, and Lenski, *Colossians*, pp. 185-86.

12. The view of Lightfoot, *Colossians*, p. 229, and Hendriksen, *Colossians*, p. 175.

earthly lords (*hoi kurioi*) of these slaves must be understood here as Christian slave owners whom Paul addressed as part of the church at Colosse. They were told to render to their slaves "that which is just and equal." The equality (*tēn isotēta*) mentioned here is probably not a demand that these owners free their slaves and thus make them social equals. The parallel passage in Ephesians required the masters to "do the same things" to their slaves as the slaves had been told to do to them (6:9), and this suggests the interpretation here. The slaves had been instructed to demonstrate the highest Christian ethics in performing their duties from the heart. The masters were now commanded to do the same in relation to their slaves. They were to treat them with justice and fairness, just as they expected to be served by their slaves. This general instruction to Christian masters is illustrated by Paul's exhortation to the slave owner Philemon, when he urged him to take back Onesimus as a "brother beloved, specially to me, but how much more unto thee, both in the flesh, and in the Lord?" (Philem. 16). The equality of spiritual brotherhood was in Paul's mind.

The whole responsibility was placed in proper perspective by Paul's reminder to the human slave lords that they also had a Lord, the one in heaven. Hence their actions were subject to scrutiny and had to meet approval, just as those of their slaves.

With these words Paul finished his exhortation to the various groups which constituted many early Christian households. The emphasis upon "the Lord" in this passage (3:18, 20, 22, 23, 24; 4:1) should remind us that our domestic life is just as sacred as our more formal "religious" activity. Every human relationship has implications for the Christian.

D. Final Exhortation to Prayer and Conduct (4:2-6)

1. Prayer to God (4:2-4)

VERSE 2. As the letter neared its close, the apostle exhorted the whole church regarding its activity toward God and toward others. The function of prayer is singled out for special emphasis. Prayer should be made with steadfast continuance. The word "continue" (KJV) or "devote yourselves to" (NASB) denotes giving constant attention to something (*proskartereite*). The Colossians' reliance upon God and looking to Him for guidance would determine their success in withstanding the false teachers in their midst.

Prayer should also be made in a spirit of watchfulness. The word *grēgoreō* literally means to be awake, to keep watch over. Figuratively it refers to spiritual alertness. When Christians pray, they must do so without divided interests or inattention. They should also be aware that opposing spiritual forces would frustrate the purposes of God wherever possible, and hence sensitivity to the fact of spiritual battle is required (Eph. 6:12, 18).

Prayer should also be made with thanksgiving. This is always to be an accompaniment of prayer (Phil. 4:6). By being conscious of what God has done for us in Christ so that we are intelligently expressing thanks to Him, we are prompted to pray regularly and without mind-wandering or spiritual dullness.

VERSE 3. The prayers of the Colossians were requested for

Fig. 11. Porta San Paola (Gate of St. Paul), Rome. Levant

certain specific matters. At the same time that they were engaged in praying, they were asked to pray "for us." The plural included Paul and Timothy and perhaps his other assistants (4:7-14). Specifically, the Colossians were to pray that God would "open up to us a door for the word" (NASB). The same expression is used in Acts 14:27 where it refers to the opening of an opportunity to Gentiles to receive the gospel. Here it refers to an opportunity for the speakers of the gospel. The "word" here is defined as "the mystery of Christ," and has been explained in 1:26-27. It was the message revealed by God that salvation is available to Jew and Gentile alike on the basis of Christ's saving work.

It was Paul's energetic proclamation of this message that had resulted in his imprisonment. Consequently he and his associates needed special divine enablement to get the gospel out. This opening of a door must not be understood merely as prayer that the prison doors might be opened for Paul. The prayer had to do not just with the prisoner Paul but also with his companions who were not prisoners ("us"). He was looking for ways to be effective even while he was a prisoner. That God answered this prayer is obvious from such passages as Acts 28:30-31 and Philippians 1:12-13.

VERSE 4. Having requested prayer that he and his associates be granted opportunity to proclaim the message of the mystery of Christ, Paul next had a more personal petition. Shifting to the singular he asked for prayer that "I may make it clear in the way I ought to speak" (NASB). Paul knew that the manner in which the gospel was presented is highly important. Perhaps he was thinking of how he would bear his witness when his case came up for trial. He was concerned that the gospel be made clear to his listeners, regardless of who they might be. Many a Roman had heard only a caricature of the Christian message. Paul's desire was that his readers at Colosse would join in prayer that God would make him effective when the door of opportunity opened.

2. Conduct toward men (4:5-6)

VERSE 5. The apostle next turned his attention to the Christian obligation toward one's fellow man. He wrote first of the believer's walk, with particular concern for Christian conduct in relation to non-Christians ("them that are without," KJV). A similar designation of unbelievers occurs in I Timothy 3:7. Christians are to conduct their lives "in wisdom," that is, to live in the light of the knowledge of God's will (1:9) and then to apply this knowledge in a practical way. Unless this is done, Christians may antagonize unbelievers through inconsiderateness or inconsistency, and do little to attract them to the gospel.

"Redeeming the time" (KJV) can be understood as "buying up the opportunity." A similar use of this expression was used in an unfavorable sense in Daniel 2:8 (LXX), where Nebuchadnezzar accused his wisemen of stalling: "I know that you are buying up time." Christians, however, are to buy up every opportunity to influence unbelievers toward God and the gospel.

VERSE 6. The believer's speech is also singled out for special exhortation. It should always be exercised "with grace." In contrast to the sins of speech which characterize the "old man" (3:8-9), Christians should continually display graciousness in their communication with non-Christians and with each other. Because of the theological prominence of the word "grace" denoting God's favor in redeeming men, it is likely that our understanding of the term here should be colored by that important concept. Our speech to others (including unbelievers) should be characterized by the same kind of grace whereby God has dealt with us. Love, patience, sacrifice, and undeserved favor are aspects of grace which our speech should display.

The Christian's speech must also be "seasoned with salt." This vivid metaphor suggests either the attractiveness of one's speech (from the use of salt to make food palatable and savory) or its wholesomeness (from the common use of salt as a preservative). In the Old Testament salt was used in the ritual of making a lasting covenant because its preserving qualities supplied an appropriate symbol of endurance (Num. 18:19; II Chron. 13:5).[13] Favoring the latter emphasis is Paul's reference elsewhere to "corrupt speech" which should not issue from the Christian's mouth (Eph. 4:29).

Finally, the believer's speech must be suited to each individ-

---

13. Friedrich Hauck, "Halas," TDNT, I, 228.

ual. Not only must the opportunity be grasped to bear an effective witness, but there must also be the use of spiritual discernment so that "ye may know how ye ought to answer every man." It is assumed that consistent Christian living in this world will create opportunities for a witness and will raise questions that deserve reasonable answers (see also I Peter 3:15). The Christian is responsible to conduct his affairs and to speak always in such a way that his life provides a consistent witness to his faith in the midst of a world that is largely unbelieving.

Questions for Discussion

1. Is Paul's instruction that wives be subject to their husbands still valid for Christians?
2. In what ways does the Women's Liberation movement contradict Scripture? In what ways does it harmonize with Scripture?
3. Is it ever right for a child to disobey his parents?
4. What is meant by being "watchful" in prayer?
5. What are some ways in which Christians should walk more wisely toward outsiders?

11

The Personal Touch

COLOSSIANS 4:7-18

The closing paragraphs of an epistle by Paul have a special fascination for the Bible student who desires an insight into the personal aspects of early Christianity. It is largely these portions of the New Testament which make it more than just a collection of theological treatises. What we have is a glimpse into the personal lives of Paul and his friends. We learn of their travels, something of their personalities, their house churches, and many other details that turn these historical names into real persons. The ending of Colossians is no exception. In it we are provided information that enlarges our understanding of the life and practice of the early church.

CONCLUSION (4:7-18)

A. Introduction of the Bearers of the Epistle (4:7-9)

1. Tychicus (4:7-8)
VERSE 7. Tychicus is no stranger to the New Testament reader. His name appears five times in association with Paul at three different stages of the apostle's career. He was from the province of Asia and accompanied Paul at the close of the third missionary journey (Acts 20:4), apparently as one of the delegates taking the collection to Jerusalem. He was with Paul in Rome toward the close of the first Roman imprisonment (Eph. 6:21; Col. 4:7). Near the end of Paul's life he was sent on missions to Crete (Titus 3:12) and Ephesus (II Tim. 4:12).

In Colossians, he was described by three phrases similar to

the description of him in Ephesians 6:21, and to that of
Epaphras (1:7). "Beloved brother" related Tychicus to all other
Christians and gave adequate reason for welcoming him to
Colosse. "Faithful minister" described him as a servant[1] (*dia-
konos*) of Christ who could be relied upon. "Fellowservant in the
Lord" tied Tychicus to Paul as being jointly with Paul in
servitude to Christ. Literally a "fellow slave" (*sundoulos*) with
Paul, the apostle acknowledged Tychicus as one who had joined
him in subjecting himself completely to the will of Christ. Paul's
function in the body of Christ may have been more prominent
than that of Tychicus, but Paul had no hesitation in placing
Tychicus in the same category with him.

It would have been the responsibility of Tychicus to relate to
the Colossians all the details about Paul's circumstances. Much
more needed to be said than could be included in a letter. Inasmuch as Tychicus was an associate of Paul, he could not only
convey information but could also properly interpret what was
happening and could explain Paul's attitudes and plans.

VERSE 8. "Whom I have sent"[2] refers not to a previous
sending but to the present instance when Tychicus would travel
from Rome to Colosse with this epistle and the one to Philemon.
He would also be delivering the Epistle to the Ephesians (Eph.
6:21-22), and perhaps one to the Laodiceans (Col. 4:16).

"That you may know about our circumstances"[3] follows the
preferred reading which agrees with Paul's declared purpose of
Tychicus' visit (4:7, 9). This statement enlarges the previous
reference ("my circumstances," 4:7). The Colossians were to be
informed not only of Paul personally, but also of Timothy and
others ("our circumstances"). In so doing, Tychicus would "en-

---

1. Although *diakonos* was also the term used in the technical sense of the office of deacon in a local congregation, it is more likely used here in the ordinary
sense of anyone who ministers or serves.

2. Paul frequently used *epempsa* or *epesteila* in this epistolary sense: II Cor.
8:18, 22; 9:3; Eph. 6:22; Phil. 2:25, 28; Philem. 12. See also Heb. 13:22. The
aorist indicative, a past tense, looks at the act from the standpoint of the reader,
not the sender.

3. The alternative reading "that he may know your circumstances" is
followed by KJV, but does not offer as good an explanation for the numerous
variants at this place. See Bruce M. Metzger, *A Textual Commentary on the
Greek New Testament* (London, 1971), p. 626.

courage your hearts," for he had good news to bring. The gospel had not been stifled in Rome (Phil. 1:12-14). Prospects for release from imprisonment were encouraging for Paul (Phil. 2:24; Philem. 22). Furthermore, the spiritual instruction Tychicus could impart through his own teaching as well as by delivery of Paul's epistle could encourage the Colossians to stand firm against the false teachers in their midst.

2. Onesimus (4:9)

VERSE 9. On the trip to Colosse, Tychicus was to be accompanied by Onesimus. A full explanation concerning Onesimus was given in the Epistle to Philemon, and Paul did not repeat it here. The Colossians had known him as an unfaithful runaway slave. Now he was introduced upon his return as "the faithful and beloved brother." These same descriptives were used of Tychicus (4:7). Paul had come to love this man, having seen what God had done in transforming him into a brother in Christ. In relating Onesimus to the Colossians, Paul said merely, "who is one of you." Much more could have been related but Paul reserved that for Philemon. Surely this was a delicate touch by one who was a master at the art of writing difficult matters in a most effective way. Because a runaway slave was in constant danger of being seized by the slave catchers, he would be traveling with Tychicus who could vouch for him.

"They will inform you about the whole situation here." Without calling attention to the fact, Paul nevertheless revealed his confidence in the reliability of Onesimus by associating him with Tychicus as jointly responsible for reporting the news from Rome. Their report would doubtless include events regarding the church at Rome, and perhaps also the story of Onesimus' conversion.

B. Greetings from Paul's Coworkers (4:10-14)

1. Jewish coworkers (4:10-11)

VERSE 10. Six of Paul's associates sent their greetings to the Colossians (five of the six are mentioned also in Philemon). The first three were Jewish Christians. Aristarchus was from Thessalonica in Macedonia (Acts 20:4), and had been unwittingly involved in the riot of the silversmiths at Ephesus (Acts

19:29). He had accompanied Paul on the voyage to Rome (Acts 27:2), and was with him at the time of this writing. Only from the present passage do we learn that he was a Jew (v. 11).

Aristarchus was called by Paul "my fellowprisoner" (*ho sunaichmalōtos mou*). Inasmuch as the term means "prisoner of war,"[4] it can hardly be understood in the literal sense here. Furthermore, it is used of Epaphras but not Aristarchus in the companion Epistle to Philemon (v. 23), the reverse of the use in Colossians. Although it is sometimes explained as a reference to a shared imprisonment with Paul, and even of a voluntary imprisonment by turns (thus accounting for the designation applied here to Aristarchus, elsewhere to Epaphras),[5] this particular word for "prisoner" is not the one to be expected.[6] Consequently it is more likely that the term is metaphorical, referring to a spiritual captivity to Christ. Paul's fondness for military figures is often seen in his letters.[7]

Mark, the cousin of Barnabas, also sent his greetings. This is the man elsewhere called John Mark (Acts 12:25). He had been a member of Paul's first missionary party, but had abandoned Paul and Barnabas during the journey (Acts 13:5, 13). An attempt to reinstate him for the second journey met with Paul's firm refusal, and caused a rupture between the apostle and Barnabas (Acts 15:37-39). Doubtless the family connection[8] between Barnabas and Mark accounted for the greater sympathy Barnabas displayed for the younger man. God apparently used both the firmness of Paul and the subsequent guidance of Barnabas to conserve Mark's gifts for the ministry. Paul was eventually reconciled to both men (I Cor. 9:6; II Tim. 4:11), and Mark was the writer of the Gospel which bears his name.

Mark was in Rome with Paul, but was planning a trip eastward which might bring him to Colosse ("if he comes to you"). Paul instructed his readers to welcome him if he should visit

---

4. Gerhard Kittel, "Aichmalōtos," TDNT, I, 195-97.

5. See T. K. Abbott, *The Epistles to the Ephesians and to the Colossians* (Edinburgh, reprinted 1974), p. 300.

6. The word *desmios* is more technically correct if a literal meaning were intended.

7. Eph. 6:11; Phil. 2:25; II Tim. 2:3; Philem. 2.

8. The word *anepsios* means "cousin." Its use as "nephew" (KJV) is later than New Testament times. Abbott, *Colossians*, p. 300.

them. Perhaps there was some prejudice against Mark in the Pauline churches because of his previous failure, but this was not to be held against him.

"About whom you received instructions" implies some prior information of which we know nothing. Had Paul previously written to the Colossians? No other hint of this appears in the epistle, and some statements in Colossians lead the reader to suppose this letter was his first communication with them (1:4, 7-8). One plausible explanation is that Paul refers to verbal directions that he was sending to the Colossians through Tychicus.[9] Thus "received" is actually another instance of an epistolary aorist (compare 3:8), referring in this instance not to any information in the present letter, but to the spoken instructions given by Tychicus at the time this letter was delivered.

VERSE 11. Jesus Justus is mentioned only here in the New Testament. Not one of the outstanding figures in biblical history, he nevertheless was a valued associate of Paul and serves as a reminder that God uses faithful persons, whether or not they achieve "star status."

These three were Paul's coworkers for the kingdom of God. Although the kingdom of God often refers to the Messianic kingdom of the future, it is used here of the present time in which the proclamation of the gospel helps to form the nucleus of the kingdom (1:13). Aristarchus, Mark, and Jesus Justus were the only Christians of Jewish descent who were then laboring with Paul at Rome in his ministry. They were certainly not the only Jewish Christians in Rome (Acts 28:24), but were Paul's only Jewish associates at the time of writing. They had provided real comfort and assistance to him at this difficult time. If this reference be regarded as a discouraging comment, perhaps it should be explained in the light of Philippians 1:15-17, where Paul noted that some Christian workers in Rome had acted shabbily toward him. It may be, however, that the mention of so few Jewish associates was to contrast the false teachers at Colosse who emphasized Judaizing practices (2:16-17). In Christ all racial barriers have been removed, and there was no need to have a predominantly Jewish group of leaders.

9. R. C. H. Lenski, *The Interpretation of St. Paul's Epistles to the Colossians, et al.* (Columbus, 1937), pp. 199-200.

2. The Colossian coworker (4:12-13)

VERSE 12. Epaphras has already been mentioned in this epistle (see 1:7). He was the one who had come to Paul at Rome
bringing word of the dangerous situation at Colosse. Although
he was "one of you," and was probably the founder of the
Colossian church, he was not returning home just yet so he sent
along his greetings. Paul designated him as a "bondslave of
Christ Jesus," a title he used often of himself, but of others only
in the case of Timothy (Phil. 1:1) and now Epaphras. This
pointed to the fact that Epaphras was not only born again but
was serving Christ completely.

Of particular interest to the Colossians would have been the
information that Epaphras had an unflagging spiritual concern for
them, even though he was at that time far away. In his prayers
he was "laboring fervently" (agōnizomenos) in their interests.
This athletic metaphor pictured the intensity of the struggle
against spiritual adversaries. With Epaphras it was both
energetic and frequent ("always"). Specifically he prayed that
the Colossians might stand firm in spite of the pressure of false
teachers. They were to be mature (teleioi), not like spiritual
babies who cannot discern truth from error and hence are tossed
about by the winds of false doctrine (see Eph. 4:13-14). This
desired maturity would display itself by their being "fully
assured[10] in all the will of God" (NASB). This lay at the heart
of their problem in Colosse. Uncertainty of God's will lays a
person open to enticement along a different path. The faithful
pastor Epaphras made it the aim of his fervent prayers that the
Colossians would be thoroughly convinced of what God had
revealed as His will for believers, and then would submit themselves totally to it.

VERSE 13. Paul adds his solemn testimony that Epaphras had
"much concern" for his spiritual flock in Colosse, Laodicea, and
Hierapolis. The word "concern" (ponon) in other literature
meant toil or labor. In the New Testament its only other uses
occur in Revelation, where it carries the idea of pain (16:10, 11;
21:4). In the present instance we should probably regard the

---

10. The verb plērophoreō can mean either to fulfill or to convince fully, and
both senses are used in the New Testament. The latter admirably fits the passage
here, and avoids tautology with teleioi.

Fig. 12. Hierapolis, ruins of theater. *Levant*

term as denoting a concern which was deep enough to cause real anguish of heart. The doctrinal threat to these churches was not taken lightly by Epaphras, and the reminder from Paul was meant to awaken the readers to the seriousness of the situation.

The neighboring cities of Laodicea and Hierapolis were located on opposite sides of the Lycus Valley, about six miles from each other and ten miles west of Colosse. It is clear that Epaphras had a special interest in all of these churches, and it is probable that he was the founder or teacher at Laodicea and Hierapolis, just as he was at Colosse (1:7).

3. Gentile coworkers (4:14)

VERSE 14. Inasmuch as these names are separated from those "of the circumcision" (4:11), Luke and Demas must be Gentiles. This passage reveals that Luke was a physician. He is mentioned by name here and in two other New Testament passages (II Tim. 4:11; Philem. 24). This man, the writer of one of the four Gospels and the Book of Acts, had accompanied Paul on parts of his second and third missionary journeys, and also on the voyage to Rome.[11] Luke had endeared himself (he is called "beloved") to Paul by his faithfulness, and he no doubt ministered to Paul's bodily needs with his professional services as a physician. It is of special interest that the writers of two of the Gospels were with Paul in Rome at the same time.[12]

Demas also sent his greetings. This is the same man who later abandoned Paul (II Tim. 4:10). At this time, however, no problems are indicated. No hint of brewing trouble should be drawn from Demas' position at the end of the list, inasmuch as the companion letter to Philemon lists him between Aristarchus and Luke and calls them all "fellow workers" (v. 24). Perhaps Demas was the amanuensis who penned the letter, and mentioned himself last and without praise.[13]

C. Final Instructions (4:15-17)

1. Greetings to various groups and persons (4:15)

VERSE 15. A request was made for the Colossians to convey Paul's greeting to the Christian brethren in Laodicea (see comments on 2:1, 4:13). This implies that there was frequent contact between these nearby churches.

Greetings also were sent to "Nympha and the church that is in her house" (NASB). The manuscripts vary between the masculine name Nymphas (adopted by KJV) and the feminine Nympha,[14] and also the pronouns "her," "his," and "their." On the assumption that the feminine Nympha is correct,[15] the greeting is understood as directed to a house church that met at the home of a Christian woman named Nympha. History

---

11. This can be deduced from the occurrence of the "we" passages in Acts, which are indications of the author's personal participation on those occasions.

12. This opportunity for contact may explain some of the similarities between the Gospels of Mark and Luke, without the need to resort to such questionable expedients as dependence upon a hypothetical "Q" or other documents.

13. This is suggested by A. S. Peake, "Colossians," EGT, III, 547.

14. The accusative case form used here is spelled the same for either, the difference being indicated only by the accent.

15. This is the reading adopted by the United Bible Societies Greek New Testament.

records no separate church buildings before the third century—until that time believers met in private homes. Other New Testament references to this practice occur in Romans 16:5, I Corinthians 16:19, and Philemon 2. It is a reminder that the physical building is not the essential factor. The church is a living organism composed of people, and its meeting place is a matter of convenience.

Where was Nympha's house church located? If it was in Colosse it was not the main Christian body there, for the Colossians are told to greet this church for Paul. A more common suggestion assigns it to Laodicea, inasmuch as the mention occurs between two references to Laodicea. If the group at Nympha's house was distinct from "the brethren who are in Laodicea," then it must have been another, perhaps smaller or newer group who regularly met together. No doubt cities had numerous groups such as this since one house would not usually be large enough for a really sizable crowd. Still another possibility is Hierapolis, for otherwise it seems strange that no greetings are sent to that city even though it is mentioned in the context.[16] Sufficient data are not available for us to be certain. (Of course, the first readers of the epistle had no difficulty, for they knew who Nympha was and where she lived!)

2. *The reading of the epistle* (4:16)

VERSE 16. When this letter to the Colossians was delivered to the appropriate church officials by Tychicus and Onesimus, it was to be read to the believers. The verb "be read" (*anagnōsthēi*) was the regular word for reading aloud, and was commonly employed of the public reading of Scripture in Jewish synagogues (Luke 4:16; Acts 13:27; 15:21). After the letter was read in Colosse, the church was responsible to send it or a copy to the church in Laodicea. Incidentally, this brief instruction indicates how the local churches obtained copies of the various New Testament writings. It probably did not take many years until at least the larger churches had secured copies of most or all of the apostolic writings.

The Colossians were also to read a letter that would be com-

---

16. R. C. H. Lenski, *Colossians*, p. 205.

ing to them from Laodicea. This "letter from Laodicea" poses
questions for the interpreter that cannot be answered with
finality, although suggestions have been many.[17] It does not
seem likely that it was a letter that the Laodiceans had written
to Paul, for if Paul had it in his possession he could have sent it
himself to the Colossians. Nor does it refer to the Latin document entitled "To the Laodiceans," which is rightly rejected as
a mere compilation of Pauline phrases, doubtless put together to
satisfy the curiosity aroused by this reference in Colossians.
Evidence is also lacking for the view that it was a letter written
by Paul from Laodicea (e.g., I Timothy, I or II Thessalonians,
Galatians). His imprisonment would have prevented his being in
Laodicea at that time, and there is no indication from Acts that
he had ever been there.

Two reasonable possibilities remain. Many explain the statement as a reference to the Epistle to the Ephesians. Because
three important manuscripts (Sinaiticus, Vaticanus, and Papyrus
46) omit the phrase "at Ephesus" in Ephesians 1:1, it is
sometimes argued that the document was intended as a circular
letter, perhaps with a space for each church to insert its name.
The reason given why most of our manuscripts have the words
"at Ephesus" is because they emanated from Ephesus, site of
the largest Christian church in the area. Colosse, however,
would have received delivery of that circular epistle by way of
Laodicea, inasmuch as Tychicus would presumably have
reached Laodicea first on his way east from Rome. Nevertheless
one wonders why greetings were sent to the Laodiceans in the
Colossian letter (4:15) if they had received their own letter from
Paul at virtually the same time. Furthermore, the other instances
of circular letters in the New Testament do not leave spaces for
names to be filled in (e.g., Galatians, I Peter, James), and
therefore another explanation should probably be sought for the
missing phrase in those three manuscripts.

The other possibility is to regard the "letter from Laodicea"
as one Paul had previously written to that church and which the

---

17. An excellent resumé, together with the Latin text, a reconstructed Greek
text, and two English versions of this work are given in J. B. Lightfoot, *St.
Paul's Epistles to the Colossians and to Philemon* (Grand Rapids, reprinted), pp.
274-300.

Colossians were to obtain and read, but which is no longer extant. Its contents were important for the immediate situation (perhaps dealing with the false teachers in the Lycus Valley), but the differences from the Colossian letter were not of universal or abiding value. This would not be the only instance of a lost letter of Paul (see I Cor. 5:9). God, who inspired the writing of the New Testament documents, also guided the preservation of the canon. If this particular letter no longer exists, we can be confident that, although it was useful at the time, God did not intend it as part of Scripture.

3. A message for Archippus (4:17)

VERSE 17. Archippus is mentioned twice in the New Testament, here and in Philemon 2. The nature of the latter reference implies that he was a member of Philemon's family, presumably a son of Philemon and Apphia. In that passage he was acknowledged by Paul as a "fellow soldier." The Colossian church was to deliver a message to Archippus that he take heed to and carry out the ministry which he had received from the Lord. We cannot be sure why this indirect approach was taken by Paul. Certainly it was not a rebuke for indolence. Paul would not have censured delinquency in such a public and embarrassing way. Nor do we know the nature of his "ministry" (*diakonian*). The term is related to the word "deacon," but it was also used in a broader sense (Acts 12:25). Perhaps Archippus had been selected by the church to take the place of its former pastor Epaphras, whether temporarily or permanently. Because of his comparative youth, he could well use encouragement by being reminded that the Lord had actually given him this ministry. It could also inspire him to renewed vigor when he saw the church which had installed him take an active interest in his God-given responsibilities.

D. A Parting Word (4:18)

VERSE 18. The body of the letter had been penned by an amanuensis, as was Paul's regular custom (Rom. 16:22). In order to insure genuineness to his readers, he signed it himself, along with a few closing remarks (see II Thess. 3:17). In his own handwriting he asked that the Colossians remember his imprisonment. He probably meant not merely recalling the fact that he was a prisoner, but remembering him in prayer that God would protect His imprisoned servant and also enable him to continue his ministry of proclaiming the gospel (4:3-4).

With the brief benediction "Grace be with you," Paul commended the Colossians to the care and protection of God's matchless grace. A proper realization of what God's grace has provided in Christ would prevent the readers from falling victim to the legalistic teachings which were the occasion for this epistle. The very survival of the letter suggests that the Colossian church heeded Paul's counsel and emerged victorious from its conflict.

Questions for Discussion

1. What are the benefits of Christians sharing experiences with each other?
2. What lessons can be learned from the relationship between Paul and Mark?
3. What were the advantages of house churches?
4. What are some disadvantages of house churches?
5. What qualities of Epaphras made him an effective leader?

The Epistle to Philemon

12

Introduction to Philemon

The beautiful letter to Philemon has special charm for the New Testament reader. Among epistles that deal with profound theological themes, church controversies, and apostolic troubles, the letter to Philemon stands out as a refreshing change of pace. It deals with a personal and private matter, and does so with remarkable charm and grace. Paul's tact and delicacy reveal an aspect of his character that many would not have suspected from the forceful and authoritative apostle. Some have wondered why such a letter was ever included as part of Scripture. Others have sought to allegorize its meaning supposing that there must be some hidden "spiritual" interpretation that would justify the inclusion of such mundane subject matter in the Bible. In so doing they often miss the message that Philemon has for the Christian believer. A careful study of this letter, however, gives the reader a glimpse into real life, with Christian principles being applied to human relations which might otherwise be far different. The Christian church is richer because of the Epistle to Philemon.

Authorship

Paul's authorship of the letter has strong attestation in early Christian history and is not doubted today by any reputable scholar. It was mentioned in the Muratorian canon (c. 170 A.D.), the collection of Marcion (c. 140 A.D.), and by Tertullian[1] and Eusebius, who placed it among the acknowledged

---

1. Tertullian, *Against Marcion*, 5:21, in *The Ante-Nicene Fathers*, ed. Alexander Roberts and James Donaldson (Grand Rapids, reprinted 1951), III, 473.

Pauline epistles.[2] It is closely linked with the Epistle to the
Colossians, being carried to Colosse by Onesimus (Philem. 10-
12), in company with Tychicus (Col. 4:7-9) who also brought the
letter to the Ephesians on the same journey from Rome (Eph.
6:21-22). Presumably any question about the genuineness of the
letter would have been noted by the church at Colosse and
would have caused its rejection from the canon. That both are
included argues that Philemon is as authentically Pauline as
Colossians.

Occasion and Date

From a reading of the letter, one learns that Paul has come in
contact with a slave Onesimus who was the property of a Christian friend at Colosse named Philemon. Whether the slave had
previously heard of Paul and sought him out, or was recognized
in the city by Tychicus and brought to Paul, is not indicated.
Through this contact Onesimus had become a Christian. His
faith in Christ was such that he apparently was ready to heed
Paul's instruction to return to Philemon and face up to his
wronged owner. To explain the situation and to appeal for a
truly Christian reception on the part of the owner Philemon,
Paul wrote this charming letter with all the sensitivity and
graciousness that one could desire. (For an alternative view,
remarkable for its ingenious reconstruction but convincing only
to a few, the reader is referred to the work of John Knox.[3])

---

2. Eusebius, *Ecclesiastical History*, 3.3,25, in *Eusebius*, trans. Hugh Jackson
Lawlor and John Ernest Leonard Oulton (London, 1972), I, 66, 86-87.

3. According to this view, the slave owner was not Philemon but Archippus
who was also the owner of the house where the church met. Paul allegedly did
not know Archippus, so Philemon was also mentioned in the greeting with the
hope that he would assist in urging compliance. Philemon is regarded as
overseer of a group of churches and was viewed as living in Laodicea. Inasmuch
as the letter would go to Laodicea and be read first by Philemon, it is to be identified as the "letter from Laodicea" (Col. 4:16). The "ministry" which Paul
asked Archippus to "fulfill" (Col. 4:17) was a request to send Onesimus back to
Paul. Knox also hypothesizes that the Onesimus mentioned by Ignatius as
bishop of Ephesus about fifty years later was the former slave, and that he was
responsible for collecting the Pauline letters, including this one. John Knox,
Philemon Among the Letters of Paul (New York, 1935). Also Edgar J.
Goodspeed, *New Solutions of New Testament Problems* (Chicago, 1927), pp.
50-64. A good critique may be found in Donald Guthrie, *New Testament Introduction, The Pauline Epistles* (Chicago, 1961), pp. 247-50.

Fig. 13. Ancient road in Rome (Decumano Massimo), the city of Paul's imprisonment. *Levant*

The date of Philemon is A.D. 60 or 61 (see chapter 1, "Introduction to Colossians," *Occasion and Date*). The epistle was written near the close of Paul's first Roman imprisonment (Philem. 22), at the same time as Ephesians and Colossians, and was delivered by Tychicus and Onesimus.

Slavery in the First Century A. D.

An understanding of the operation of slavery in the Greco-Roman world is essential if one is to view Paul's statements from the proper perspective. Paul wrote from the standpoint of one who knew well what Old Testament teaching and Jewish practice was, and he was thoroughly conversant with the way the institution functioned in the Gentile world. Only if these factors are the controlling ones in our understanding can we avoid imposing present day "civil rights" issues back upon an earlier culture where they may not be relevant.

Slavery was taken for granted in all of ancient society. It was recognized under the Mosaic law, but was carefully safeguarded against abuse. A Jewish slave could not be held more than six years (Exod. 21:2). A Jew could sell himself into slavery, but even in such cases he had to be released after fifty years of bondage (Lev. 25:39-42). Special procedures had to be followed if perpetual voluntary service were desired by the slave (Exod. 21:5-6; Deut. 15:16-17). Slaves who had been maimed by their masters could be set free (Exod. 21:26-27). The murder of a slave was punishable by death (Exod. 21:12). Hebrew slaves could marry, although if the master had provided a wife, the wife and children remained the property of the owner when the slave was released (Exod. 21:4).

Slavery in the Roman Empire could be considerably harsher than under the Mosaic law. However, one must not generalize from the cases of outrageous abuse which have been publicized, and erroneously suppose that such were typical of first-century practice. Previously the chief source of slaves had been capture in war or kidnapping by pirates.[4] After the cessation of the wars of conquest and the establishment of law and order, the primary source for slaves was internal, and chiefly through breeding. Children born to slave mothers were themselves slaves. Abandoned children were also usually raised as slaves.[5] Furthermore, many people sold themselves into slavery, often in order to better themselves.[6] It has been estimated that one-third of the population of the city of Rome was enslaved,[7] and this estimate is probably true for other parts of the empire as well.

The difference between an average urban slave and a poor freeman was more a matter of principle than of practice.[8] It is true that a slave was virtually powerless in any legal sense. Yet

---

4. S. Scott Bartchy, *Mallon Chrēsai: First-Century Slavery and the Interpretation of I Corinthians 7:21*, in Society of Biblical Literature, Dissertation Series, Number Eleven (Missoula, Montana, 1973), p. 45.

5. Ibid.

6. Ibid.

7. Barker, G. W., Lane, W. L., and Michaels, J. R., *The New Testament Speaks* (New York, 1969), p. 211.

8. S. Scott Bartchy, *First-Century Slavery*, p. 115.

if he were part of an urban household, he was often above the lowest dregs of society.[9] He had a certain physical security in his position, and could even accumulate some money toward a *peculium*, the growing sum with which he would later hope to buy his freedom.[10] Such slaves functioned as clerks, accountants, doctors, nurses, teachers, advisors, musicians, and artists.[11] For various reasons, therefore, a poor freeman might sell himself into slavery in order to better his status. The money he received for so doing could be set aside for his peculium; his owner would be responsible for his material needs, and upon eventually receiving his freedom, he could expect to be made a citizen.[12] A poor freeman, on the other hand, had no job security. A capable slave was often given an excellent education, and was entrusted with important responsibilities. Evidence from tombstone inscriptions indicates the high regard in which some slaves were held.[13]

Furthermore, the prospect of securing manumission (legal release) was a realistic expectation in the first century. Owners often held out this hope as an incentive for better work, and it thereby served the owner's advantage. A person under normal circumstances could count on serving ten to twenty years after his maturity before being set free.[14] Records exist indicating great frequency of manumission during this period.[15]

Runaway slaves were treated severely by Roman law, and owners were allowed great latitude in punishing the recaptured fugitive. It was common to brand him on the forehead with an "F" (for *Fugitivus*), or even to kill him. If a master was a Roman citizen, the law required that a heavy penalty (50,000 sesterces) be paid to him by anyone who concealed the runaway, and the wages or services owed during the slave's absence were required from the one who concealed him. On the

---

9. Ibid., p. 61.

10. Ibid., p. 47.

11. Ibid., p. 68; Barker, Lane, Michaels, *The New Testament Speaks*, p. 211.

12. S. Scott Bartchy, *First-Century Slavery*, p. 117; R. H. Barrow, *Slavery in the Roman Empire* (New York, reprinted 1968), pp. 173-74.

13. Ibid., p. 70.

14. Ibid., p. 83.

15. A Rupprecht, "Slave, Slavery," *The Zondervan Pictorial Encyclopedia of the Bible*, ed. Merrill C. Tenney (Grand Rapids, 1975), V, 458-59.

other hand, if the master was a provincial, a Roman citizen (such as Paul) was not legally obligated to return a slave who had sought refuge with him.[16] Inasmuch as the status of Philemon is not known, Paul's legal obligations regarding Onesimus cannot be fully assessed.

It should not be concluded that the slave's lot during the first century was an easy one. Those who were assigned to work the mines, engage in heavy construction, or man the galleys (often these were criminals) had a wretched existence. It is a mistake, however, to imagine that all slaves in the empire were seething with unrest, awaiting the moment to revolt. The last serious slave rebellion occurred 130 years before Paul wrote to Philemon.[17] Slavery was accepted as a part of the economic and social life of the ancient world. Abuses were committed; many of the worst ones were recognized as such and made illegal. Rarely, however, was the institution of slavery itself debated. The New Testament nowhere denounces the system, but rather insists upon the demonstration of genuine Christian ethics by every party involved. Each believer, whether slave or master, is responsible to the same Lord in heaven, is an equal member of the body of Christ, and has the obligation to display Christian love and consideration to every other believer. Differences in social status are incidental; what is vital is the oneness of all believers in Christ.

Special Features

1. The Epistle to Philemon is the only Pauline letter of the New Testament which deals with an entirely private matter. Several other letters by Paul were addressed to individuals (Timothy, Titus), but they included discussions requiring church action. Philemon is similar to II and III John in its personal character.

2. This epistle gives the clearest New Testament illustration of the master-slave relationship in the early church.

---

16. Barker, Lane, Michaels, *The New Testament Speaks*, pp. 212-13; S. Scott Bartchy, *First-Century Slavery*, p. 15; P. R. Coleman-Norton, "Paul and the Roman Law of Slavery," *Studies in Roman Economic and Social History* (Princeton, 1951), pp. 173-74.

17. The revolt led by Spartacus in 70 B.C.

3. Paul's tact and delicacy in dealing with a potentially explosive issue is beautifully presented.

4. Apphia and Philemon are mentioned only here in the New Testament.

The Outline of Philemon

Greeting (1-3)
  A. The Writer (1a)
  B. The Addressees (1b-3)
I. Thanksgiving and Prayer for Philemon (4-7)
  A. The Occasion (4-5)
  B. The Request (6)
  C. The Explanation (7)
II. Plea for Onesimus (8-21)
  A. Basis of the Plea (8-9)
  B. Subject of the Plea (10-11)
  C. The Explanation (12-16)
  D. The Request (17)
  E. Paul's Offer (18-20)
  F. Paul's Confidence (21)
III. Concluding Matters (22-25)
  A. Request for a Lodging (22)
  B. Greetings from Paul's Associates (23-24)
  C. Final Blessing (25)

EXPOSITION
OF
PHILEMON

GREETING (1-3)

A. The Writer (1a)

VERSE 1a. This is the only epistle of Paul in which he describes himself in the opening greeting as "a prisoner of Christ Jesus." He has apparently chosen to lay aside his usual title "apostle," which might have seemed too official for this personal appeal, or "bondservant," which stressed his function as one of service to Christ. He selected instead the expression "prisoner," not merely in the sense that every believer has been captured by Christ's love (for Paul never used the term when he was free), but because he was literally confined at the time of writing. Nevertheless, he was not complaining that he was a prisoner of Rome, but regarded his jailing as part of his ministry in the cause of Christ whom he delighted to serve (Acts 9:16).

"Timothy the brother" is joined with the name of Paul as a courtesy inasmuch as Timothy was with Paul at this time and was apparently known to Philemon (see comments on Colossians 1:1). Timothy had been present during part of Paul's three-year stay in Ephesus, and could have become acquainted with Philemon's household at that time (Acts 19:22). Paul, however, is the sole writer of the epistle (note the pronouns "I," "me," or "my" in every verse from 4 to 24, except verse 15).

B. The Addressees (1b-3)

VERSE 1b. The addressee Philemon is not otherwise known to us. He is here termed a "beloved one" and a "fellow worker" of Paul and Timothy, one who had endeared himself to the apostle and had worked with him and others in the Christian ministry. This does not necessarily mean that he was a preacher in any formal sense (although he may have been). From this letter we learn that he had opened his home as a meeting place for the church, and perhaps had been active in furthering the gospel witness in Colosse. The letter further reveals Philemon to be a slaveowner who had been wronged by a slave named Onesimus.

VERSE 2. Although the letter is obviously directed to one person (note the singular "you" in verses 4, 5, 6, 7, 8, 10, 11, 12, 13, 14, 15, 16, 17, 18, 19, 20, 21, 22[verb], 23), two other individuals are included in the address. "Apphia the sister"[18] is apparently a family member (otherwise she probably would have been listed after Archippus), and presumably was the wife of Philemon. "Archippus our fellow soldier" is certainly to be identified with the man named in Colossians 4:17 as having a ministry at Colosse or in a neighboring city. He may have been

---

18. The reading "beloved Apphia" (KJV) is found in the textus receptus, but is not supported by those manuscripts most highly regarded today.

the pastor of the church at Colosse after the departure of Epaphras for Rome (Col. 1:7; 4:12). Since the church at Colosse had been sent its own letter, it is somewhat strange to find this reference to Archippus in the salutation to Philemon unless he were also a member of the household. Consequently, it is not unlikely that Archippus was the son of Philemon and Apphia, but was also a stalwart Christian whom Paul was happy to acknowledge as a fellow sharer of the dangers and hardships of the Christian ministry.

"And to the church in your house" reflects the early Christian existence of house-churches before the rise of separate church buildings (see on Col. 4:15). Philemon's house was the meeting place for the Colossian congregation (or one of its congregations). The inclusion of the church in the greeting was an indication that the matter to be discussed in this letter would have relevance for the entire local church. The return of Onesimus could not go unnoticed. Whatever was done should be clearly understood by the whole congregation.

VERSE 3. The blessing pronounced upon Philemon and his household is the same as that bestowed upon the Colossians (see comments on Col. 1:2), except that the name of the Lord Jesus Christ is added. In these twin blessings of grace and peace, the familiar Greek and Hebrew greetings are combined and adapted into a most meaningful Christian benediction.

I. THANKSGIVING AND PRAYER FOR PHILEMON (4-7)

A. The Occasion (4-5)

VERSE 4. As was usual with Paul, he moved into the body of the letter with a thanksgiving to God regarding matters pertaining to his readers.[19] An indication of Paul's spiritual greatness was his habit of looking at everything from God's perspective and finding something for which to be thankful. The incidental mention of "my" God reveals how personal and real his relationship was.

"Always" makes better sense if it is connected with "give

---

19. The exceptions are II Corinthians, Galatians, I Timothy, and Titus.

thanks" (as in NASB), rather than with "making mention" (KJV). It was hardly true that Paul was always mentioning Philemon in his prayers, but it is readily understandable that he was always thanking God for Philemon whenever he did mention him. An accurate translation is: "I thank my God always while making mention of you in my prayers."

VERSE 5. This thanksgiving for Philemon was caused[20] by information Paul had heard, probably from Epaphras (Col. 1:7-8), and perhaps confirmed by Onesimus after his conversion had provided him with a new perspective.

What Paul had heard was a report of Philemon's love and faith—basic qualities that characterize the genuine and maturing Christian. The next two phrases can be understood in several ways. The faith is stated as being directed toward the Lord Jesus. If both love and faith are to be interpreted as focused on the Lord, are we also to understand that "to all the saints" marks an additional object of Philemon's love and faith? There is no problem in understanding love as having this two-fold direction, but it is hardly conceivable that Paul would place faith in Christ and faith in the saints on an equal plane. ("Saints" is a frequent New Testament designation for all believers.) For this reason it is sometimes urged that *pistin* should be understood here in the sense of faithfulness or fidelity, rather than faith. However, the word is never used in this sense in the New Testament when it is joined with "love," or when it appears in the expression "to have faith."[21]

The best explanation understands Paul's thought as moving from Philemon's love to his faith in Christ which prompted it, and then he comes full circle and completes the reference to love by naming its immediate object—his fellow believers, It is an example of the literary device called *chiasmus*, in which two pairs are listed in parallel relation, with the second pair in reverse order. Thus item 2 corresponds to item 3, and item 4 relates to item 1. The effect is a criss-cross, suggesting of the Greek letter *chi* (X) which lends its name to the construction. It can be depicted as follows:

20. Causal use of the circumstantial participle *akouōn* (hearing).
21. M. R. Vincent, *The Epistles to the Philippians and to Philemon* in The International Critical Commentary series (Edinburgh, reprinted 1972), p. 179.

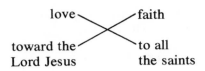

The use of different Greek prepositions in these phrases intimates that there is a different relation being expressed (*pros, eis*). The most compelling reason for preferring this view is Paul's use elsewhere of the concepts "faith in Jesus" and "love to all the saints" without the complicating problem of chiasmus (Eph. 1:15; Col. 1:4).

B. The Request (6)

VERSE 6. As Paul prayed for Philemon (v. 4), he desired that "the fellowship (*koinōnia*) of your faith may become effective." This brief clause is difficult to interpret because the word *koinōnia* has a number of different uses. In the present instance, the probable choices can be narrowed to two. Did Paul mean that Philemon's "participation in the faith" (i.e., his status as a Christian) was to be increasingly displayed? Or was Paul asking that Philemon's "sharing with others as an outgrowth of his faith" become energetic? Both ideas are legitimately drawn from the grammar and are appropriate to the context. Paul's ultimate hope was that Philemon would demonstrate his Christian faith and love in the specific matter of Onesimus, although he had not yet mentioned his name in the letter. Favoring the view that the more active "sharing" concept should be understood, rather than just Philemon's membership (participation) in the Christian body, is the parallel Pauline thought using similar wording in Philippians 1:5 ("your fellowship with reference to the gospel"), and II Corinthians 8:4 ("the fellowship of ministering to the saints").

This active demonstration of Christian fellowship would come about "in full knowledge of every good thing which is in us with reference to Christ" (literal). "In" (*en*) is instrumental here: "by or through full knowledge. . . ." As Philemon increasingly recognized all the spiritual realities that Christ had provided in salvation, he would be stimulated to display a similar sort of grace to the undeserving Onesimus.

C. The Explanation (7)

VERSE 7. Paul explained why he was always thankful in his remembrance of Philemon and could pray so confidently for him along the lines of verse 6. It was because Philemon had already displayed true Christian charity and generosity. Paul had received "much joy and encouragement" from the report of Philemon's "love" when Epaphras had conveyed information to him in Rome (Col. 1:8). A believer, and especially a Christian leader, is always encouraged when he learns that a convert is growing in his spiritual capacity and is displaying the fruit of the Spirit in his relations with others. In the case of Philemon his love and faith had already brought refreshment to the hearts[22] of the believers[23] in Colosse. Paul had made previous reference to this fact (v. 5), and his prayer was that Philemon's sense of fellowship would become large enough to include Onesimus, of whom he was about to speak.

The statement concludes with the warm, affectionate address, "brother." The reality of the Christian *koinōnia* has constituted each believer a brother to every other member of the body of Christ. The mention of this relationship would surely have brought Philemon renewed rejoicing as he basked in the glow of Paul's written acknowledgment of him as a brother. He was soon to learn that Paul wanted him to do the same for Onesimus (v. 16).

Questions for Discussion

1. What features of the Epistle to Philemon impress you?
2. What are the implications of the phrase, "the fellowship of your faith"?
3. How does Paul expect Philemon's increased display of fellowship to be motivated?

---

22. See chapter 9, note 13.
23. Greek: *hagiōn* (saints), one of the common New Testament designations of believers.

4. What are some ways in which Christians can refresh the hearts of other Christians?
5. What admirable characteristics of the man Philemon are reflected in this passage?

13

A Plea for a Friend

PHILEMON 8-25

The very year[1] in which Paul wrote to Philemon, there was born a man who became the distinguished Pliny the Younger, a Roman lawyer, writer, and orator, whose surviving letters fill many volumes. On one occasion Pliny wrote to a friend named Sabinianus, and the reason for his letter was strikingly similar to the Epistle to Philemon.

TO SABINIANUS

Your freedman, whom you lately mentioned as having displeased you, has been with me; he threw himself at my feet and clung there with as much submission as he could have done at yours. He earnestly requested me with many tears, and even with the eloquence of silent sorrow, to intercede for him; in short, he convinced me by his whole behavior, that he sincerely repents of his fault. And I am persuaded he is thoroughly reformed, because he seems entirely sensible of his delinquency.

I know you are angry with him, and I know too, it is not without reason; but clemency can never exert itself with more applause, than when there is the justest cause for resentment. You once had an affection for this man, and, I hope, you will have again; in the meanwhile, let me only prevail with you to pardon him. If he should incur your displeasure hereafter, you will have so much the stronger plea in excuse for your anger, as you show yourself more exorable to him now. Allow something to his youth, to his tears, and to your own natural mildness of temper: do not make him uneasy any longer, and I will add too, do not make yourself so; for a man of your benevolence of heart cannot be angry without feeling great uneasiness.

---

1. Approximately. Pliny the Younger was born in A.D. 61 or 62.

I am afraid, were I to join my entreaties with his, I should seem rather to compel, than request you to forgive him. Yet I will not scruple to do it; and so much the more fully and freely as I have very sharply and severely reproved him, positively threatening never to interpose again in his behalf. But though it was proper to say this to him, in order to make him more fearful of offending, I do not say it to you. I may, perhaps, again have occasion to intreat you upon his account, and again obtain your forgiveness; supposing, I mean, his error should be such as may become me to intercede for, and you to pardon. Farewell.[2]

Pliny was not a Christian, though as governor of Bithynia under the emperor Trajan in the second century he once commented on the peculiar practices of Christians in his territory. Many aspects of his letter to Sabinianus remind us of Philemon, but there is not much likelihood that Pliny ever saw Paul's letter. Beautiful as his letter was, it fell short of the exalted appeal by Paul, because it never rose above the level of a merely human friendship. Paul's plea for Onesimus, however, was raised to the highest spiritual plane, being grounded on the fact that regeneration in Christ has made believers "brothers."

II. PLEA FOR ONESIMUS (8-21)

A. Basis of the Plea (8-9)

VERSE 8. The word "wherefore" supplies a transition, referring to the statements immediately preceding regarding the evidence of Philemon's genuine love for others. Even though[3] Paul did not lack courage to use his apostolic authority and command the appropriate action from Philemon, this time he proceeded by a different route. His confidence in his authority was, however, well founded, for it was "in Christ." His commission by Christ made him an apostle, and this gave him a special position in God's spiritual household (Eph. 2:20).

Nevertheless Paul had no egotistical pride in his apostolic rank, and did not demand that men always defer to his dignity.

---

2. Pliny, *Letters*, Book 9, Letter 21, trans. William Melmoth, in the Loeb Classical Library (London, reprinted 1927), II, 221-23.

3. The circumstantial participle *echōn* (having) is concessive: "although I have."

When the occasion required it, such as in the defense of true doctrine, he would insist upon his authority to declare the truth (Gal. 1—2). With Philemon, however, Paul took a different tack because he knew that Philemon was noted for his sensitivity to the demands of love (verses 5, 7).

VERSE 9. It is on account of the love that is produced by the Spirit in the hearts of Christians, a love already displayed by Philemon, that Paul based his plea. He was confident that this approach, rather than the issuing of a command, would be effective.

At the same time he reminded Philemon who it was that was making the plea. It was Paul, "an old man, and now also a prisoner." Several reasons have been suggested why "old man" (*presbutēs*) should be translated instead as "ambassador" (*presbeutēs*). Lightfoot argued that the second "e" was sometimes omitted from *presbeutēs*, so that the reading in the text *presbutēs* can still mean "ambassador."[4] This meaning would then be an interesting parallel with another Pauline statement, "I am an ambassador in chains" (Eph. 6:20). Furthermore, Paul was called a "young man" (*neanias*) in Acts 7:58, and it seems unlikely that at this time he could have been more than fifty-five years old, hardly any older than Philemon himself. Why then would he mention it?

However, favoring the rendering "old man" are the following factors which seem decisive. 1) It is preferable to take the simpler, more usual meaning of the word, rather than adopt an irregular spelling of "ambassador." 2) Paul's experiences involved hardships which would have aged him prematurely, a factor which Philemon probably knew well. 3) "Old man" fits the context better than "ambassador," for Paul is making a fatherly plea for his young convert. If "ambassador" were the meaning, Paul's plea would be based on his office and authority, the very fact he has just denied.

To the description "old man" Paul added the mention of his circumstance as "a prisoner of Christ Jesus." Though a prisoner at Rome, he dignified it by relating it to his commission from

---

4. J. B. Lightfoot, *St. Paul's Epistles to the Colossians and to Philemon* (Grand Rapids, reprinted), pp. 338-39.

Christ (Acts 9:15-16). These two designations—old man and prisoner of Christ Jesus—should have stirred the Christian love of Philemon into alertness and prompt operation.

B. Subject of the Plea (10-11)

VERSE 10. It should be remembered that Onesimus has not yet been mentioned in the letter, and his name is delayed until the very last word of verse 10 (as in NASB). Paul wanted to lay a foundation for his request before mentioning the name that would certainly raise unpleasant memories.

As he moves toward the identification Paul first designated him as "my own child." The expression "my own" (*emou*) is stronger than "my" (*mou*) would have been, and clearly associated Paul himself with the life and fortunes of Onesimus. He then explained how this relationship of child and father came about. It was not by natural birth, but was the new birth which occurred when Paul had won him to Christ during the present imprisonment. Hence Paul was appealing for a Christian whom he had personally won to the Lord in the least likely circumstances—his own imprisonment.

Finally the name Onesimus is given. The name itself meant "useful, profitable," and was a common one for slaves. Whether Onesimus was standing before Philemon with trepidation awaiting his reading of the letter, or whether he was outside so that Philemon had no hint of what was coming in the letter can only be guessed. Either way Paul has done everything possible to make Philemon favorably disposed, by stating that this Onesimus was his own child, and had become such during his long and irksome imprisonment.

VERSE 11. Having now identified the subject of his plea, Paul proceeded to acknowledge the previous failures of his convert, but he did so with a play on words that provided a light touch at a crucial moment in the appeal: "who formerly was useless [*achrēston*] to you, but now is useful [*euchrēston*]." Both adjectives are from the same root with different prefixes (in Greek) altering their meanings.[5] While Onesimus was absent from his

---

5. It is possible that an even more subtle pun is to be seen in the fact that *euchrēston* (useful) is a synonym of the name Onesimus, although normally a pun must use a form of the same word or at least one which sounds similar.

master, he was obviously of no use to him whatever. Perhaps his service had also been less-than-acceptable even before his departure. Now Paul could assert that Onesimus is a useful man, both to Philemon and to Paul. He had doubtless already demonstrated a changed life by assisting Paul in various ways (see v. 13). Upon his return to Philemon, Onesimus would perform faithfully, not merely with eyeservice (Col. 3:22).

C. The Explanation (12-16)

VERSE 12. Having stated that he was appealing on the basis of love regarding Onesimus, Paul then proceeded to give a fuller explanation of the circumstances which had prompted this plea. A great many textual variants occur here among the manuscripts, but a literal rendering of the preferred text is as follows: ". . . whom I have sent back to you, him, that is, my own heart." The verb is another Pauline instance of an epistolary aorist, referring not to some prior sending but to the present occasion viewed by the writer as it will appear to the reader (see note on Col. 4:8).

It had been no easy matter for Paul to send Onesimus away. He had become deeply attached to him, and was doubtless concerned as always about bringing this new believer to maturity (Col. 1:28). To sever that close relationship was a wrenching experience for the apostle. It was like sending away a vital part of himself—"my own heart."

VERSE 13. So strongly was he drawn to Onesimus that he said of him, ". . . whom I could have wished to retain to myself." The verb "wished" (*eboulomēn*) employs the imperfect tense to describe action going on in the past but not completed. It depicts here a tentative or potential purpose which was not completed because it was replaced by another action. Paul's wanting to retain Onesimus never became a fully-resolved intention because it was stopped and replaced by the decision explained in verse 14. "I could have wished" conveys the thought fairly well.

Onesimus could have been useful to Paul during the remaining weeks of his imprisonment. Already he had shown his helpfulness during the first days of his contact with the apostle. Paul understood, of course, that Onesimus belonged to Philemon, and if he should stay in Rome his ministering to Paul would be as Philemon's representative ("in thy stead"). "The bonds of the gospel" is a reference to the imprisonment which had its origin[6] in the gospel which Paul preached.

VERSE 14. The apostle was quick to add that his wish to retain the services of Onesimus was meant only to show what a valuable man this convert had become. It was not to be interpreted as a serious attempt to keep him in Rome. The statement, "I wished to do nothing without your consent" uses a verb in the aorist tense[7] to indicate the decisive act which put an end to the previous inclinations. He did not want a "good act"[8] of Philemon, such as letting Paul have the services of Onesimus, to seem forced in any way.

The use of "as it were" utilizes the comparative conjunction in the common classical sense with prepositional phrases with the meaning "as if."[9] Not only would Philemon's granting of Onesimus to Paul have had to be "not by compulsion," but "not as if by compulsion." It could not have had even the appearance of being forced. If Philemon had ever wanted to send Onesimus to Paul, it would have been appreciated, but the whole matter would have had to originate with Philemon himself, without a suggestion from Paul. Hence we cannot suppose this to be a hint that Paul would have liked Onesimus sent back to him. After stating the above thought to Philemon, Paul could hardly have then accepted the favor.

VERSE 15. This further suggestion to Philemon encouraged him to look at the whole incident from the broadest possible perspective; namely, the providence of God. "Perhaps" introduces the thought delicately so as not to offend Philemon, and possibly also to reflect the fact that Paul himself did not claim complete knowledge of all God's ways. Nevertheless, he suggested that God may have had a direct hand in what had happened and had used it to accomplish a greater good. To describe Onesimus' flight as "he was parted" (rather than "he parted himself" or

---

6. *Tou euangeliou* is a genitive of origin, as in Col. 1:23, denoting the source from which Paul's bonds had come.

7. Greek: *ethelesa*.

8. Greek: *to agathon sou*.

9. For two other New Testament instances, see II Cor. 11:17 and II Thess. 2:2.

"he fled") suggested that beyond Onesimus' own schemes a higher power was operating. "For a while" (lit. "for an hour") is in contrast to "forever." However many weeks or months the flight to Rome had taken, it was short in comparison to the eternal relationship which had now been established between Philemon and Onesimus.

VERSE 16. Not only was it in God's providence that Philemon should get Onesimus back forever, but also that he should be "no longer as a slave." The importance of "as" (*hōs*) should be noted. Paul did not say "no longer a slave," thereby stating that Onesimus must be freed, but "no longer as a slave." This referred to the manner in which Philemon was to regard him. The sense is: "no longer as a mere slave, even though he may still have that legal status." Onesimus now possessed an additional quality. He was a "brother beloved," because he had been born again into the family of God and was a Christian brother to every other believer.

His relationship as a beloved brother had a special significance for Paul ("especially to me"), who had been God's instrument to lead Onesimus to Christ. Yet from another standpoint Philemon had even more reason to regard Onesimus with warmth and affection ("how much more to you"), because he was receiving back his slave who would now render more conscientious service ("in the flesh") as well as one who could share with him spiritually in true Christian fellowship ("and in the Lord").

D. The Request (17)

VERSE 17. Here Paul makes his actual request of Philemon: "Receive him as you would me" (NASB). All of the preceding material in the epistle has been laying the groundwork. Paul has shown that Onesimus has become a true sharer of the Christian faith, a fact which has brought him into fellowship with Paul, his spiritual father, and with every other Christian. The apostle, however, does not unduly strain Philemon's graciousness by basing his appeal on the new but untested merits of Onesimus, but on the relationship between Philemon and Paul: "if then you regard me a partner." Certainly there is no reason to doubt that Philemon counted Paul as a sharer along with himself of the vital union that makes all believers one with Christ and hence partners (*koinōnon*) with each other. Just as Philemon would have welcomed Paul as a Christian brother if he visited Colosse (v. 22), so Paul asked that he show the same sort of welcome to Onesimus.

E. Paul's Offer (18-20)

VERSE 18. Lest Philemon hesitate to accede immediately to Paul's request because of some "unfinished business" with Onesimus, the apostle hastened to remove a final obstacle. "If he has wronged you in any way or owes" is another conditional clause. By the use of "if," Paul avoided speaking bluntly of possible theft, and left the way open for Philemon to claim what he considered right. It is sometimes suggested that the mere absence of Onesimus was the only wrong in view, and the debt consisted of the lost time involved. However, this does not explain the presence of the word "if." There was nothing "iffy" about Onesimus' absence, and thus it is better to suppose at least the possibility of theft, perhaps to finance the runaway's flight to Rome. Pilfering was a common vice of slaves (Titus 2:10).

"Charge this to me," said Paul, using a technical commercial term for charging to an account.[10] He offered to pay in full whatever charges Philemon wanted to assess against Onesimus.

It is unwarranted to imagine that Paul was without funds and thus could not really have assumed such an obligation. If that were the case, this would have been a meaningless offer and such gestures are insulting rather than gracious. Actually little is known about Paul's finances at this time. He must, however, have had access to some funds in order to finance his appeal to Caesar. Furthermore, he hoped for release in the near future and would presumably be working to support himself as he had done in the past (Acts 18:3; 20:33-35). By whatever means he envisioned for payment, Paul offered to assume the indebtedness of Onesimus if Philemon could reckon it in money.

VERSE 19. Paul insisted that his offer to repay was valid by pointing to the fact that he had affixed his own signature to it: "I

---

10. Herbert Preisker, "Ellogeō," TDNT, II, 516-17.

Paul have written[11] with my own hand: I will repay." It is sometimes concluded that at this juncture the apostle took the pen from the amanuensis and wrote these words himself. However, the almost incidental way in which the statement occurs in the paragraph makes it more likely that he actually penned the whole letter. Although this was a departure from his usual practice of using an amanuensis, the personal nature of the letter easily accounts for his doing so.

Paul's statement sounds like a formal promissory note, although one may doubt whether he meant it as a purely legal document. Nevertheless he did mean to stand behind his word; if Philemon was in financial straits and needed help, Paul intended to make the repayment.

Fig. 14. First century papyrus containing handwritten promise to repay. Deissmann, *Light from the Ancient East*, p. 331.

---

11. The verb *egrapsa* is an epistolary aorist.

The additional remark, "that I may not say to you that you owe to me even your own self as well," was a reminder that Philemon himself was deeply indebted to Paul. It was by Paul's ministry, whether directly or indirectly (through Epaphras perhaps), that Philemon's conversion to Christ had occurred. Thus Philemon was doubly indebted to Paul—for the return of Onesimus in far better condition than before, and for his own salvation. The remark was made in such a way that Paul revealed his reticence even in the mention. His point was that he would not press upon Philemon all the claims that he might, but would base his appeal only upon what he had already said. He would not stress the fact of Philemon's own debt. Hendriksen suggests that this may be an instance of Paul's fatherly humor.[12]

Paul's offer to take upon himself the full obligation of Onesimus, not because of any merits of the slave but due solely to the graciousness of the benefactor, is a beautiful illustration of what Christ has done for sinners. As Martin Luther put it in lines well worth repeating: "What Christ has done for us with God the Father, that St. Paul does also for Onesimus with Philemon. . . . For we are all his Onesimuses if we believe."[13]

VERSE 20. "Yea, brother," confirms the request made in verse 17, but the rest of the statement makes it emphatic that Paul was virtually substituting himself for Onesimus. "I would be helped by you in the Lord." The pronoun "I" is emphatic in the sentence. It was not merely Onesimus who would be helped by Philemon's favorable reception of him; it was Paul himself who so regarded it. The apostle's own heart would be refreshed as he knew that these two converts had entered into a relationship of true Christian brotherhood, in deed as well as principle.

Inasmuch as the form "I would be helped" (*onaimēn*) is also the root of the name Onesimus (*Onēsimos*), it is possible that Paul has made another play on words, although admittedly the

12. William Hendriksen, *Exposition of Colossians and Philemon* (Grand Rapids, 1964), p. 223.
13. Martin Luther, "Preface to the Epistle of St. Paul to Philemon, 1546 (1522)," in *Luther's Works*, Vol. 35, ed. E. Theodore Bachmann (Philadelphia, 1960), p. 390.

name at verse 10 is at a considerable distance. H. C. G. Moule states the pun as follows: "Let me get help as well as you get Helpful."[14]

F. Paul's Confidence (21)

VERSE 21. The "obedience" Paul mentioned is best understood as compliance with the request to receive Onesimus as though he were the apostle himself (rather than as obedience to an order, for Paul has not issued any commands to Philemon). Paul was confident that Philemon would respond favorably, and for this reason he had written the letter.[15]

The expectation that Philemon would do "even more" than had been requested has raised questions as to what Paul had in mind. Was this a veiled hint that Philemon should grant Onesimus his freedom?[16] This must remain a possibility, but it is certainly not the only way Paul's words may be taken. Nowhere else does Scripture tell Christian slave owners to release their slaves. Some suggest that Paul wanted Onesimus sent back to Rome to be his assistant.[17] However, Paul would hardly have sent Onesimus on the arduous journey to Colosse if he expected him to come back immediately. Furthermore, such an action would directly contradict Paul's stated purpose of avoiding anything that even remotely appeared to be less than Philemon's own free choice (v. 14). Also, Paul expected to be leaving Rome himself shortly (v. 22), and thus the return of Onesimus to Rome was hardly his thought. Far more likely is the view that explains "even more" as Philemon's wholehearted and energetic response to Paul's request, rather than a mere perfunctory compliance.[18] Paul knew his man, and was confident that when all the facts were known Philemon's welcome would be even warmer than he had been able to suggest.

---

14. H. C. G. Moule, *Colossian and Philemon Studies* (London, n.d.), p. 311 footnote.
15. Another instance of *egrapsa* as an epistolary aorist.
16. J. B. Lightfoot, *Colossians and Philemon*, p. 345.
17. John Knox, *Philemon Among the Letters of Paul* (New York, 1935), pp. 22-32, 69-70.
18. William Hendriksen, *Exposition of Colossians and Philemon*, p. 224.

III. CONCLUDING MATTERS (22-25)

A. Request for a Lodging (22)

VERSE 22. At the same time that Philemon was receiving
Onesimus, Paul wanted him to begin making arrangements for
his own arrival. He knew that the prayers of many, including the
family of Philemon and the church at his house ("your" is a
plural form), had been offered on his behalf. The legal charges
against him were flimsy (Acts 23:29; 24:13; 25:25-27; 26:31-32),
and therefore he expected to be released when his case was
finally settled (Phil. 2:24). His purpose to visit Spain (Rom.
15:24) may have been changed or delayed to allow this eastward
trip. Many years and unforeseen events had occurred since that
earlier plan was stated.

The present tense of the imperative verb "prepare" (lit.
"engage in preparing") may imply that there was no special
hurry, but that preliminary steps could be taken. When Paul
traveled, it was usually with a party of associates and the task of
preparing accommodations was greater than simply providing a
guest room for the apostle.

B. Greetings from Paul's Associates (23-24)

VERSE 23. The first greetings came from Epaphras, the
evangelizer of Colosse and presumably their recent pastor (Col.
1:7). He is termed by Paul "my fellow prisoner," the same
designation as used of Aristarchus in Colossians 4:10 (see comments). The literal meaning "war captive" (*sunaichmalōtos*)
cannot be meant; therefore, the description must be figurative of
his willing servitude to Christ in the spiritual warfare which Paul
and he were waging.

VERSE 24. The remaining four names were mentioned also in
Colossians (where an additional name, Jesus Justus, was in-
cluded[19]). The first two, Mark and Aristarchus, were Jewish
Christians (see Col. 4:10 and context). Demas and Luke were

---

19. Perhaps Jesus Justice was a Roman Christian who sent his greetings in a
general way to the entire church at Colosse, but was omitted in this listing
because he was not personally acquainted with Philemon.

Gentiles (as their mention in Col. 4:14 indicates by separating them from those of the circumcision). At this time the whole group were "fellow workers." Later Demas forsook Paul (II Tim. 4:10), but Luke was faithful to the end (II Tim. 4:11).

C. Final Blessing (25)

VERSE 25. With Paul's familiar benediction, "The grace of the Lord Jesus Christ be with your spirit," his lovely letter comes to its close. "Your" is a plural form, showing that the apostle has broadened his scope from Philemon alone, who had been the focus of the main part of the epistle, to all of those who had been addressed in the intial greeting (vv. 1-2). We possess no sequel to this letter to indicate the outcome. The fact, however, that Philemon preserved his epistle for the benefit of Christians everywhere strongly suggests that he fulfilled Paul's expectations. May such displays of Christian grace be the aspiration of all who claim to know the love of Christ.

Questions for Discussion

1. On what did Paul base his appeal to Philemon?
2. What instances of Paul's tact do you find in this letter?
3. Do you think Paul was asking Philemon to release Onesimus? Why or why not?
4. Could Paul the prisoner have actually carried out his offer of verses 18-19?
5. In what ways did Paul exemplify Christ's dealings with sinners?
6. What implications do you see in this passage for modern social problems?

Bibliography

Abbott, T. K. *Epistles to the Ephesians and to the Colossians* in the International Critical Commentary series. Edinburgh: T. and T. Clark, reprinted 1974.

Arndt, W. F., and Gingrich, F. W. *A Greek-English Lexicon of the New Testament.* Chicago: University of Chicago Press, 1957.

Barker, G. W., Lane, W. L., and Michaels, J. R. *The New Testament Speaks.* New York: Harper and Row, 1969.

Barrow, R. H. *Slavery in the Roman Empire.* New York: Barnes and Noble, Inc., reprinted 1968.

Bartchy, S. Scott. *Mallon Chrēsai: First-Century Slavery and the Interpretation of I Corinthians 7:21*, in Society of Biblical Literature, Dissertation Series, Number Eleven, 1973.

Carson, Herbert M. *The Epistles of Paul to the Colossians and Philemon* in the Tyndale New Testament Commentaries series. Grand Rapids: Wm. B. Eerdmans Publishing Co., 1960.

Coleman-Norton, P. R. "The Apostle Paul and the Roman Law of Slavery," *Studies in Roman Economic and Social History*, ed., P. R. Coleman-Norton. Princeton: Princeton University Press, 1951.

Dana, H. C., and Mantey, J. R. *A Manual Grammar of the Greek New Testament.* New York: The Macmillan Co., 1946.

Deissmann, Adolph. *Light from the Ancient East.* Grand Rapids: Baker Book House, reprinted 1978.

Erdman, Charles R. *The Epistles of Paul to the Colossians and to Philemon.* Philadelphia: The Westminster Press, 1933.

Eusebius. *Ecclesiastical History* in *Eusebius.* Translated by Hugh Jackson Lawlor and John Ernest Leonard Oulton. London: Society for Promoting Christian Knowledge, 1927.

Francis, F. O. "Colossians," *The Interpreter's Dictionary of the Bible, Supplementary Volume*, ed. Keith Krim. Nashville: Abingdon, 1976.

Goodspeed, Edgar J. *New Solutions of New Testament Problems*. Chicago: University of Chicago Press, 1972.

Guthrie, Donald. *New Testament Introduction, The Pauline Epistles*. Chicago: InterVarsity Press, 1961.

Harrison, Everett F. *Introduction to the New Testament*. Grand Rapids: Wm. B. Eerdmans Publishing Co., 1971.

Hendriksen, William. *Exposition of Colossians and Philemon* in New Testament Commentary series. Grand Rapids: Baker Book House, 1964.

Herodotus, trans. A. D. Godley, in the Loeb Classical Library. New York: G. P. Putnam's Sons, 1922.

Herodotus. *The Histories*. Translated by Aubrey de Selincourt. Middlesex: Penguin Books, 1972.

Hiebert, D. Edmond. *Titus and Philemon* in Everyman's Bible Commentary series. Chicago: Moody Press, 1957.

Irenaeus. *Against Heresies*, in *Ante-Nicene Fathers*, ed. Alexander Roberts and James Donaldson. Grand Rapids: Wm. B. Eerdmans Publishing Co., reprinted 1950.

Johnson, S. Lewis. "Christ Preeminent," *Bibliotheca Sacra*. 119:473 (January, 1962).

_____. "Christian Apparel," *Bibliotheca Sacra*. 121:481 (January, 1964).

_____. "From Enmity to Amity," *Bibliotheca Sacra*. 119:474 (April, 1962).

Josephus. *Antiquities of the Jews*. Translated by Louis H. Feldman, in the Loeb Classical Library. Cambridge: Harvard University Press, 1965.

Josephus. *Jewish Antiquities*. Translated by Ralph Marcus, in the Loeb Classical Library. Cambridge: Harvard University Press, 1937.

Kent, Wendell E. "The Spoiling of Principalities and Powers," *Grace Journal*. Vol. 3, No. 1 (Winter, 1962).

Kittel, Gerhard, and Friedrich, Gerhard, eds. *Theological Dictionary of the New Testament*. Translated by Geoffrey W. Bromiley. Grand Rapids: Wm. B. Eerdmans Publishing Co., 1964-72.

Knox, John. *Philemon Among the Letters of Paul*. New York: Abingdon Press, 1935.

Lenski, R. C. H. *The Interpretation of St. Paul's Epistles to the Colossians, to the Thessalonians, to Timothy, to Titus and to Philemon*. Columbus: Wartburg Press, 1946.

Liddell, H. G., and Scott, R, revised by H. S. Jones. *A Greek-English Lexicon*. Oxford: Oxford University Press, n. d.

Lightfoot, J. B. *St. Paul's Epistles to the Colossians and to Philemon*. Grand Rapids: Zondervan Publishing House, reprinted.

Luther's Works, Volume 35, *Word of Sacrament I*, ed. E. Theodore Bachmann. Philadelphia: Fortress Press, 1960.

Luther's Works, ed. Jaroslav Pelikan and Walter Hansen, Volume 29, *Lectures on Titus, Philemon, and Hebrews*. St. Louis: Concordia Publishing House, 1968.

Metzger, Bruce M. *A Textual Commentary on the Greek New Testament*. London: United Bible Societies, 1971.

Moule, Handley C. G. *Colossian and Philemon Studies*. London: Pickering and Inglis Ltd., n. d.

Moulton, J. H. *A Grammar of New Testament Greek, Prolegomena*. Edinburgh: T. and T. Clark, 1908.

Muller, Jacobus J. *The Epistles of Paul to the Philippians and to Philemon*, in the New International Commentary series. Grand Rapids: Wm. B. Eerdmans Publishing Co., 1955.

Oesterley, W. E. "The Epistle to Philemon," *The Expositor's Greek Testament*, ed. W. Robertson Nicoll. Grand Rapids: Wm. B. Eerdmans Publishing Co., reprint edition.

Peake, A. S. "The Epistle to the Colossians," *The Expositor's Greek Testament*, ed. W. Robertson Nicoll. Grand Rapids: Wm. B. Eerdmans Publishing Co., reprint edition.

Pliny. *Letters*. Translated by William Melmoth in the Loeb Classical Library. London: William Heinemann, reprinted 1927.

Ramsay, William M. *St. Paul the Traveller and the Roman Citizen*. Grand Rapids: Baker Book House, reprinted 1949.

_____. *The Teaching of Paul in Terms of the Present Day*. London: Hodder and Stoughton, 1913.

Robertson, Archibald T. *Word Pictures in the New Testament*. New York: Harper and Brothers Publishers, 1931.

Rupprecht, A. "Slave, Slavery," *The Zondervan Pictorial Encyclopedia of the Bible*, ed. Merrill C. Tenney, Grand Rapids: Zondervan Publishing House, 1975.

Simpson, E. K., and Bruce, F. F. *Commentary on the Epistles to the Ephesians and the Colossians*, in the New International Commentary series. Grand Rapids: Eerdmans Publishing Co., 1957.

Strabo. *The Geography*. Translated by Horace L. Jones in The Loeb Classical Library. New York: G. P. Putnam's Sons, 1928.

Tacitus. *The Annals*. Translated by John Jackson in the Loeb Classical Library. Cambridge: Harvard University Press, reprinted 1962.

Tertullian. *Against Marcion. The Ante-Nicene Fathers*, eds. Alexander Roberts and James Donaldson. Grand Rapids: Wm. B. Eerdmans Publishing Co., reprinted 1951.

Van Oosterzee, Dr. "Epistle to Philemon," *Commentary on the Holy Scriptures*, ed. John Peter Lange. Grand Rapids: Zondervan Publishing House, reprinted, n. d.

Vincent, Marvin R. *The Epistles to the Philippians and to Philemon*, in the International Critical Commentary series. Edinburgh: T. and T. Clark, reprinted 1972.

The Wycliffe Historical Geography of Bible Lands, ed. Charles F. Pfeiffer and Howard F. Vos. Chicago: Moody Press, 1967.

Xenophon. *Anabasis*. Translated by Carleton W. Brownson, in the Loeb Classical Library. New York: G. P. Putnam's Sons, 1920.